The Director of Ceremonies

Charles J. Carter

LEWIS MASONIC

All royalties from the sale of this
book have been donated to the
Masonic Trust for Girls and Boys
1990 Festival
held under the auspices of the
Province of West Kent.

First published in England in 1989
by Lewis Masonic, Ian Allan Regalia Ltd
Terminal House, Shepperton, TW17 8AS who
are members of the Ian Allan Group

British Library Cataloguing in Publication Data
Carter, Charles
The director of ceremonies.
1. Great Britain. Freemasons. Lodges, Directors
of ceremonies. Duties
I. Title
366'.1

ISBN 0-85318-170-5

Contents

Foreword

HAVING HAD a close affinity with the work of a Director of Ceremonies at various levels for many years I have read this book with particular interest.

It will, I am sure, become an invaluable aid as a book of reference for both those holding the office of Director of Ceremonies and the considerable number who aspire to it.

The style, as one would expect, is positive and constructive. The chapters are arranged in a logical way providing both a general view of the particular subject and detailed suggestions for its successful implementation in the most practical way.

Every aspect of this most important office is covered and discussed, and the author's wide experience at different levels is more than evident.

This book will provide enjoyable and interesting reading for those who have held this office and will provide considerable food for thought for all. For those who will take on the duties of Director of Ceremonies in the future it will provide a detailed guide on every aspect on their new found responsibilities and will rapidly be established as the standard work on this most important office in every lodge.

I congratulate the author on filling a most important gap in Freemasonry. I am sure there will be many who will be eternally grateful for this book of reference who will find that there is scarcely a case of difficulty which can occur which this book will not set them right.

Simon F.N. Waley, M.A.
Provincial Grand Master – West Kent.

About The Author

CHARLES JAMES CARTER was initiated into the Three Pillars Lodge No 4923 in May 1962, became Master in 1971 and Secretary the following year. In 1971 he became Founding Secretary of the Plantagenets Lodge No 8409 in the Province of Kent and Master in 1973. He served the office of Preceptor and Director of Ceremonies for ten years.

In 1977 he was promoted to Provincial Deputy Director of Ceremonies a rank he was to hold for ten years before being promoted to Assistant Provincial Grand Master (West Kent) in 1987.

He is a member of several lodges and Chapters in Kent including the West Kent Provincial Grand Stewards' Lodge No 8565 (eight years as Director of Ceremonies); he is a founder and the present secretary of the Fiennes Cornwallis Lodge No 9279, the executive Lodge for the Province of West Kent. He was appointed to the rank of Past Assistant Grand Director of Ceremonies in 1981 and promoted to Past Senior Grand Deacon in 1988.

He is the current secretary of the Quatuor Coronati Correspondence Circle Limited, London, where he is responsible for the worldwide operations of the Correspondence Circle of the Quatuor Coronari Lodge, the premier Lodge of Research in the world.

Chapter One

Why Ceremonial?

FEW WOULD deny that the ceremonial we use in our Lodges comes directly or indirectly from that used at Court in ancient times, being altered, amended, adapted or otherwise changed to suit differing times and requirements. If we look at the great State occasions such as the opening of Parliament, the Coronation of a new Monarch, or the reception of a visiting Head of State, we see very clearly that such important events call for much planning, organisation, rehearsal and sculpting to the requirements of the occasion. Such we would suggest are the reasons why ceremonial is used, to make certain that our ceremonies are conducted with dignity, decorum and a general sense of well-being, whereby all concerned with the occasion are aware in advance of what will happen, where it will happen, when it will happen and by whom. Thus it is that our important meetings are carried through without confusion and with considerable dignity and efficiency.

The first Grand Director of Ceremonies, Sir George Nayler (1764–1831), was a member of the College of Arms. He became Blanc Coursier Herald having been appointed by the then Duke of Norfolk on 15 June 1792, and in 1793 he became Bluemantle Pursuivant, was promoted Clarenceaux King-of-Arms in 1820 and was again promoted to Garter King-of-Arms on 11 May 1822. Another Grand Director of Ceremonies, who served in the office for forty-four years, was Sir Albert W. Woods. He also was Garter King-of-Arms.

There can be no doubt at all that both of these brethren would have brought to the office of Grand Director of Ceremonies in the United Grand Lodge of England much of that ceremonial used by their forebears which, together with their College of Arms connection and involvement, may well have done much to fashion the style and manner in which we carry through the ceremonial in use to this day.

Some present-day Ceremonial is of relatively recent origin, and with small but important alterations it continues to change to meet the needs of the occasion, thus keeping abreast of current thinking and demands.

A well-run lodge meeting gains considerably, both from its content and the manner in which the various segments are drawn together by the means of ceremonial, thus providing its participants and onlookers with a relaxed, confident atmosphere in which to carry out those planned duties.

It should now be stated, and stated very clearly in this first Chapter, that the ideal Director of Ceremonies is one who controls, without perhaps more than a glance, nod or slight movement of the hand or head.

Those Directors of Ceremonies, and we all know at least one, who are far too obvious in both their presence, their intrusion, and their desire to let everyone see that they, and not the Master, are in charge are to be deprecated.

The Director of Ceremonies is an adjunct to, not a replacement for the Master, in matters of control in the Lodge. Understandably new Masters are unlikely to want to disagree with a Director of Ceremonies of many years standing particularly if he is, as are so many, also the Preceptor of the Lodge of Instruction.

It must be remembered throughout the reading of this book that a good Director of Ceremonies is not an obvious Director of Ceremonies. He should endeavour to be one of whom we are probably totally unaware but who nevertheless has complete control of the meeting at all times.

Ceremonial, when used in Freemasonry, should produce a well-run, well organised meeting, moving from segment to segment with a smooth unhurried demeanour, thus creating a relaxed and enjoyable occasion.

Chapter Two

Organisation and Preparation

CLEARLY WE must examine the total area of operation of the Director of Ceremonies; his role encompasses the supervision of the Tyler, in other words the responsibility for the correct laying out of the Lodge, the work of the Officers of the Lodge, particularly the Assistant Director of Ceremonies, the Deacons, and the Inner Guard. Before we look at these in detail it is essential that the Director of Ceremonies and the Secretary are able to work together. Ideally they should speak to each other a few days prior to every meeting to ensure that all the Officers will be present; if there should be any notified as being absent then clearly it is the duty of the Director of Ceremonies to ensure that a capable replacement is chosen, is advised, and appraised of what he has to do. The Secretary should then be advised before the meeting of the new arrangements made. It is imperative for the smooth running of any lodge meeting that the Secretary and Director of Ceremonies keep each other advised at all times of items of importance relative to the particular meeting.

Taking these duties one at a time let us start with the Tyler. An incorrect but commonly held belief is that the Tyler is RESPONSIBLE for the correct laying out of the Lodge; such however is definitely not the case. Certainly the Tyler performs the task but the responsibility for the Lodge is that of the Director of Ceremonies. He should always have a Check List made out for each degree so that he can ensure he has all the required appurtenances necessary for carrying out the degree or degrees to be worked and for the Lodge meeting in general. To assist new Directors of Ceremonies, four lists are given which will suffice in general terms; they may not of course cover the vagaries of every individual lodge working under the Constitutions of the United Grand Lodge of England. Space has been left at the end of each check list for the reader to amend it to suit his own requirements.

Starting with the Tyler, the Director of Ceremonies should, in order to give his duty an unhurried presentation, attend at least forty five minutes prior to the advised start of the meeting. He should then undertake an organised and thorough look at the Lodge room to make certain that the Tyler has carried out his duties correctly.

Is the Master's pedestal correctly laid out? Is the V.S.L. the right way round for your Lodge? Are the Square & Compasses correctly placed on the top of the V.S.L.? Is the gavel in place? Does the Master require a glass of water? Which ceremony is being performed and are the compasses or square required? Is the heavy maul in place? Has the Tyler ensured that the ribbon in the V.S.L. is in the right place? Have the working tools been properly placed and are all the working tools in the box? Will the candles last throughout the meeting?

Is the Warrant ready for the Master to take into the Lodge, with him together with the latest Book of *Constitutions* and the By-Laws of the Lodge? Are the Tracing Boards in the correct order? Is the Junior Warden's pedestal correctly laid out? Are all the required items in place to perform the ceremony? Is the Senior Warden's pedestal correctly laid out? Does the Senior Warden in your lodge have the required aprons beneath his pedestal ready for investiture and if not are they readily available near to the seat of the Director of Ceremonies for ease of collection and presentation during the ceremony?

On the Secretary's table, is the Ballot Box ready? Are the Ballot Balls in place? Are slips of paper available if a ballot by this method is to be held? Has the Charity Column been placed on the table? If there is to be an Initiation has the dish to be proffered to the candidate been placed ready for handing to the Junior Deacon at the correct part of the ceremony?

Has the Tyler ensured that there are matches available inside the Lodge for the candles to be lit both at the start of the ceremony and later if there is to be a third degree conducted?

Has the Tyler prepared the items for use with the Candidate or Candidates? Does the Tyler have the copy of the Lodge summons with the Candidate or Candidates' correct names ready for announcing to the Inner Guard? Has the Secretary prepared the Declaration Book for signature by the Candidate or Candidates? Are all the collars for the Officers of the Lodge correctly laid out either inside or outside the Lodge for the recipients to use? Is a Third Degree sheet needed for this meeting? If yes then has it been folded properly so that when the appropriate time arrives it can be placed with the minimum of fuss and time wasting? Are the wands for the Director of Ceremonies, Assistant Director of Ceremonies, and Deacons ready and waiting? Are the kneeling stools in place? Do please ensure that the Doves on the Deacons wands are held in the correct manner with the Doves flying forwards.

The guests: is there a visiting Grand Officer? Is there an Official representative from the Province or District attending the meeting and if so has a seat been reserved for him in the East? Has the Initiate invited any guests and who has been detailed to make certain they are properly greeted and tested, then looked after during their visit?

Ensure that the Assistant Director of Ceremonies also attends some forty five minutes prior to the start in order that you can instruct him in the duties you wish him to perform during that meeting. Decide which of you will escort to their seats those brethren who arrive after the start. A good division of duty and one frequently used in the better organised lodge is for the Director of Ceremonies to attend upon Worshipful Brethren and above and the Assistant Director of Ceremonies to attend upon lay brethren. Those who arrive late *MUST* be told which degree the lodge is in when greeted at the door, in order that they may give the correct sign on entering the Temple. If a visitor is received the name of his host should be elicited and after being welcomed by the Master he should then be seated as near to his host as is practicable.

Starting a meeting on time is essential. If the Lodge is scheduled to open at five o'clock then the incoming procession, if one is formed in your lodge, should be ready a full five minutes beforehand so that the meeting commences exactly on time.

It is not only discourteous to the Master and the Visiting Brethren but also gives the lodge a very bad image for a meeting to start later than the scheduled time. A very good practice and one adopted in many lodges is for the Officers to be summoned to be in attendance on the Master some fifteen minutes prior to the opening.

An Officer of the Lodge has a *DUTY* to be in attendance on the Master prior to the advised starting time of the meeting, as well as being proficient in the duties of his office.

Chapter Three

Rehearsing

THERE NEVER has been, and there never will be, any ceremony no matter how well performed which cannot be improved by rehearsal.

The majority of lodges manage to rehearse their forthcoming ceremonies at their weekly Lodge of Instruction; such rehearsals are conducted under the control of the Preceptor of the Lodge of Instruction which in many cases is the Director of Ceremonies of the Lodge. Such duplication of offices is to be welcomed, for the weekly opportunity to inspect, appraise, correct faults and generally superintend the overall performance of the officers of the lodge ensures a continuity of training and ongoing interest and rehearsal.

A good Preceptor will always find time at the end of a Lodge of Instruction to select some part of the ceremony and show the members attending the correct way to carry out some action or other. For example the correct way to control the candidate by placing one's left arm UNDER the Candidate's right arm thus controlling his arm movement in a firm but friendly manner.

Lodges of Instruction should never be places of ridicule. All who attend are without doubt trying to do their best, they come to learn and experiment, mistakes are to be expected, that is the reason for the member coming, because he is not sure and wishes to receive instruction.

The well organised Preceptor will always arrange that an annual plan of rehearsals is prepared and distributed well in advance of the start of the new season. This preplanning has many advantages for the member and the Preceptor alike. For the member it allows him to know well in advance of the occasion precisely what office he is to fill and what will be demanded of him on that night. For the Preceptor it ensures the complete team of officers for a given evening is advised well in advance, together with the part each will play. He can then make certain that as the various officers move up through the Deacons' and Wardens' offices in the Lodge each is given an increasing opportunity to fill the role of Master as each of the degrees is rehearsed.

For those Preceptors who do not already use this system but might wish to do so a chart is included at the end of this book to assist with the planning of the year's work at the Lodge of Instruction.

Chapter Four

Timing

LISTEN TO any successful after dinner speaker, any accomplished comedian or any politician of repute and you will quickly come to realise what is meant by the heading of this Chapter.

Learning to speak the written word by heart in an accurate and meaningful way is of course highly desirable, and indeed very necessary, if we are to impress on candidates the solemnity and meaning of the ceremony in which they are participating. Accuracy is one thing, delivery is entirely another; timing, when combined in a skilled manner with delivery can alter a ceremony delivered without feeling into an occasion to be remembered by all who attended, as well as being totally meaningful to the Candidate.

There should never be an occasion when it is necessary to rush a ceremony; the requirement to finish a ceremony within a given time frame is to be strongly deprecated. Each Master or Past Master will deliver a ceremony in his own individual style. Some simply use their normal speaking voice to deliver what is a highly personal ceremony whilst others give the ceremony the benefit of timing and feeling, with voice intonation, tone, pace, and volume, all helping considerably to give the various parts of the ceremony both meaning and depth.

Those who are charged with the training of brethren should remember constantly that a ceremony delivered with feeling, warmth and sincerity, albeit not necessarily word perfect, is to be preferred to a monosyllabic delivery that is word perfect but is given in an unfeeling impersonal and detached manner.

If you doubt the truth of that statement, listen carefully to that after dinner speaker, that comedian, that politician and I am sure that you will very soon agree with the truth of the saying 'It's not what you say, it's the way that you say it'.

At any meeting of a Lodge the Officers and members will

undoubtedly turn to the Director of Ceremonies when a problem arises and it is vital that he not only has the answer but maintains an aura of complete calm and total confidence for if he does not he can, and probably will, undermine the entire meeting. If you look calm and organised and behave in a calm and organised manner, you will instill calm and confidence in all those who have a part to play in the events of the afternoon and evening.

Chapter Five

Checking & Thinking Ahead

SIMPLE WORDS but without doubt words which are the secret to any well run ceremony. We have already gone through the list of items to be checked in the Lodge which must be done at every meeting, but there remains yet another sphere of checking for the Director of Ceremonies to undertake. An example perhaps might help to illustrate what is meant by the heading of this chapter. A second degree is scheduled; ten minutes before the meeting a message arrives, the candidate, cannot attend! Do you know the name of the next Candidate in order of seniority who can be asked to step into the role and be passed at this meeting rather than at the meeting at which he was scheduled to be passed? Do you know whether he has the ability to answer the questions? Do you know if he is attending today? If the answer to any of these questions is NO then you are not Checking and Thinking Ahead you are waiting for the accident to happen and then trying to minimize the damage.

Chapter Six

The Lodge of Instruction

REFERENCE HAS been made to the Lodge of Instruction earlier in this book but we shall now deal with the subject in the fullest meaning of the phrase.

What exactly should a Lodge of Instruction set out to accomplish? Is it simply to train brethren in the art and science of delivering the three degrees of craft masonry in such a proficient manner as to be the envy of all who listen? Or could it possibly be that the Lodge of Instruction has a much wider application to share with those who attend?

What should a brother attending a Lodge of Instruction hope to achieve as a result? Is the Lodge of Instruction simply in existence for the learning of words parrot fashion? Does it in fact exist to give the members the opportunity to get to know each other rather better than is possible at a normal Lodge meeting? Is it perhaps the place to learn a little more in general terms about the basis and history of the ancient Craft and why it continues to exist after hundreds of years?

The answer is probably all of those things to a greater or lesser degree, for anyone attending a Lodge of Instruction will take from his membership of it those things he wishes to take knowingly or unknowingly.

The meaning and purpose of membership of the Craft is to any member a multiplicity of history, dedication, application and on occasions a large and unanswerable proportion of Why?

Many seasoned brethren, who have been members for more years than they care to remember, will find it very hard to tell you why they travel from one end of the country to the other to attend their lodge when it is only going to carry out a ceremony they have seen hundreds of times before.

Yes it is indeed difficult if not impossible to quantify what one obtains from membership. If there is an answer to even a portion of that question then the Lodge of Instruction must go a long way to providing that answer. For that is the one place where, with patience, courtesy, attention to detail and a genuine desire to learn and understand the ritual one can see transformations take place each week.

Many brethren belong to lodges and enjoy the friendship and happiness which are part of every lodge meeting and its subsequent festive board but show little or no interest in the ritual or any desire to learn it. They are still members of the Craft, perhaps not such involved members but members nevertheless. Why then have a Lodge of Instruction? The Lodge after all can perfectly well survive without one can it not?

Someone once described the Lodge of Instruction and its relationship to the Lodge in terms of a beautiful flower, the outside being the part that is on show whilst the growing takes place out of view.

The Lodge meeting of course is where the finished and polished article is put on view for all to see whilst the Lodge of Instruction is where the growing takes place, out of sight of those who will view the final finished product.

How then can we make quite sure that we run the ideal Lodge of Instruction in which every member receives the maximum help and encouragement and the brethren look forward to the next meeting with an air of intense enthusiasm and dedication?

To try to put together the essential ingredients of this ideal place of learning let us imagine that we are in the unusual position of setting up a Lodge of Instruction where not one member has attended before. What then should we be seeking to achieve by the formation of this new and as yet totally unproven entity?

We have already established that it is advisable to have a full plan for the year with each officer marked showing in advance which office he will be required to fill on each and every evening that the Lodge of Instruction meets.

If A.B.C. etc. are used in place of the names on the chart then the chart will suffice for year after year, the names of the brethren can then be varied each year by giving each one a new letter reference which will apply to them throughout that season of the Lodge of Instruction.

We have now established what we shall be doing at each meeting and who will be filling each office. The next task will be an evaluation of the potential of each officer and the amount that he can reasonably be expected to accomplish during the coming year.

For the ease of over-viewing what has to be accomplished by brethren wishing to proceed through the offices and into the Master's chair a chart has been provided at the back of this book in order that a newly enrolled member can take a long hard look at what should be encompassed each year if he is to arrive at the day of his Installation with a complete knowledge of the ceremonies he will have to conduct together with the knowledge of the control and behaviour of the Brethren at the Festive Board, as well as a good understanding of the *Book of Constitutions*.

The efficient Master is the one who thought very deeply many years ago about his progress and planned accordingly so that he had a steady and regular pattern of achievement at which to aim and thereby arrived at his Mastership, properly trained, fully relaxed, and totally in control of any situation that might arise during his year in the chair. Yes, it can be done but not by thinking about it when you are about to be appointed as a Warden in the Lodge, because by that time it is far too late.

At our first Lodge of Instruction meeting it is very important that we explain to the assembled brethren the future format of the weekly rehearsal and what we shall be endeavouring to achieve at our meetings. We must explain to everyone present that each member will progress at his own pace and that none will receive a public admonition for his work should it prove to be below the standard expected nor for that matter, will anyone be asked to undertake a role which he feels is completely beyond him to carry out.

Above all we should make it perfectly clear that this Lodge of Instruction must be a happy occasion at which brethren will seek to improve their performance and everyone present will in all probability be doing so at an entirely different speed from his neighbour.

Whilst on this subject the Preceptor should not forget that these same remarks will require to be made to each new member of the Lodge of Instruction when he attends for the first time after his Initiation.

At our first Lodge of Instruction we shall establish that in addition to carrying out a ceremony of Initiation, time will be set aside each week for a small demonstration of the practical application of such things as how to carry a wand correctly, how to change the Tracing Boards with the maximum of polish and precision, and how the two Deacons should work together to ensure a cohesive collaboration of effort and ability.

The maximum respect is given willingly to the Preceptor who is prepared not just to tell others how to do something but is prepared to go out on to the Lodge floor and demonstrate to the brethren those things he wishes done and the manner in which such movements are to be carried out and why. A short explanation of this type each week will do much to build in the mind and knowledge of the brother regularly attending the reason why we carry out a certain action rather than doing something because he has been told to do so.

We said earlier in Chapter Three that no ceremony, however well carried out is so good that it cannot be improved by rehearsal. Rehearsal is of course why the Lodge of Instruction exists.

It certainly does not exist for the benefit of the Preceptor, to enable him to show to the lay brethren just how clever he is and how lacking in knowledge they are!

We have now rehearsed our ceremony of Initiation at our first meeting and the various points which require correction have been mentioned in a gentle and caring manner together with perhaps the demonstration we mentioned having taking place. This is now the time to mention what we shall be rehearsing next week and also to gain the assurance from the brethren who are scheduled to carry out the various offices that they will be in attendance.

Finally this must be the moment to offer congratulations to those who have attended the meeting of the Lodge of Instruction and acted in the various offices. Perhaps if one brother has done particularly well he may be mentioned by name although it is usually better to have a private word with anyone doing particularly well as indeed you would offer words of support to those who are obviously disappointed with their own performance.

Such must be the format of the meetings of the Lodge of Instruction that they will grow in strength particularly if we always remember that the Preceptor is a very special office to hold in the Lodge of Instruction.

The successful Preceptor can encourage and nurture the aspirations of the younger Brethren whilst the dominating and the authoritarian Preceptor can undermine the confidence of the younger Brother and damage his efforts to improve.

The new and inexperienced Brother in his first year of masonic life is a very precious as well as impressionable entity and must be treated with all the care that would be given to a newly created plant, for with care it will blossom and grow; without that care its future, to say the least, is very uncertain, and it could well die.

Lodges of Instruction have a secondary and very important role to perform and it is important that Preceptors and those charged with the teaching of Brethren should recognise that the newly introduced Brother will have a myriad of questions which require answers. It is at this time in his masonic career that he can be led seriously astray if he is not correctly informed by having his questions accurately and fully answered.

If, occasionally, we find we have a Brother who has asked a question to which we have no ready answer, what do we do? Should we admit that we do not know the answer or guess at what sounds like a logical, suitable, and reasonable reply? The correct response of course is to say 'I do not know the answer to that question but I will endeavour to get an answer for you by the time we meet next week'. Who knows you may well learn something yourself as the Preceptor and one should never be ashamed to admit that. The important thing is that you do give him an answer.

If the occasion lends itself and time permits it is a very useful practice for the Preceptor to explain to the Brethren assembled why we carry out certain practices in the Lodge and to explain for example the content of the ceremony of Initiation ie. the candidate is admitted knowing nothing, seeing nothing and requiring assistance at all times.

From this state of helplessness he is advanced to a position of sight and thence to an explanation of his Initiation; signs, grips and tokens are exchanged, he is presented to the Wardens, finally being invested with his Apron.

The whole ceremony is one of progression impacting on the candidate in a demonstrably meaningful manner. The reasoning behind such an explanation is that if the members of the Lodge of Instruction can get firmly fixed in their minds the various segments which go towards the making of a ceremony they will, the more readily, come to understand why certain things occur at certain times in certain Ceremonies.

Then should the occasion ever arise when they forget what comes next they can think of the Ceremony in its several parts and quickly regain their momentum and place in the Ceremony being conducted.

Finally to all Preceptors, may you always remember that evening when you were first asked to take an office in the Lodge of Instruction and in particular remember just how very nervous you felt. Times change but the feelings of Brethren are as acute today as ever they were and we must ensure that we never embarrass anyone in our enthusiasm or desire to 'break them in'.

A well run Lodge of Instruction will not only build the Brother but will build the Lodge as well and all members of the Lodge should remember that the Lodge of Instruction is where the Master of tomorrow is learning his work today.

The Lodge of Instruction is the greenhouse of the Lodge, it is where the seed is germinated, the growing takes place, and the final product is ready to take its place in the order of things.

We should also remember that, as in the greenhouse, occasionally we lose a tender plant for a variety of reasons and from this we must all learn and reduce that rare and sad occurrence to the minimum.

Chapter Seven

Grand Officers

MUCH has been written elsewhere in this book about Grand Officers and the manner in which they should be treated, saluted, cared for and generally looked after when visiting a lodge. There are however a number of small points which it is well worth mentioning at this stage of the book.

Grand Officers by their very appointment to that rank are senior members of the Craft. They will have given many years of service to the Craft, visited many lodges, watched changes take place in both the way the Craft is perceived by the general public and has altered internally. They will also have considerable experience of the ways in which lodges have changed in many of their practices over the years.

In many cases you will have available not only the experience of years, but the opportunity to look, compare, recount, and receive valuable advice when you have a Grand Officer visit your Lodge. They are simply not appointed without very adequate references and proof of much wide experience gained over many years. In most cases they will have had a much wider masonic career and experience than anyone else in your lodge. They will, in some cases. have been appointed to carry out specific tasks.

In Provinces and Districts, Grand Officers are used very widely for the purpose of visiting lodges on an annual basis usually but not necessarily at Installation Meetings, in order that a regular annual report of the state of that lodge can be recorded at the Provincial or District Office.

Grand Officers are appointed from amongst those who have given selfless service to the Craft above and beyond the call of duty and as such they should be accorded the respect and dignity which their rank demands.

If your Lodge should be fortunate in finding that one of its members has been so appointed it will undoubtedly be an occasion for celebration and rejoicing. Cherish the brother so appointed for he will have thoroughly deserved the honour as well as your respect and affection.

Grand Officers will be appointed to a given rank within the list stated at rule 5 in the *Book of Constitutions*. It is as well for the efficiency of the Lodge if the Director of Ceremonies commits to memory the ranks and their grading within that list. So that when and if a Grand Officer should appear after the start of a meeting, who is perhaps not expected, he can be seated according to his rank even if it means moving Grand Officers of lower rank, and can then be treated accordingly from that point onwards.

Grand Officers themselves will be well aware of their position in the heirachy and probably will automatically move their place in the seating if a Grand Officer of senior rank should enter. The Lodge Director of Ceremonies needs to be well versed in such protocol for these occasionally required pieces of knowledge can make the difference between panic and calm in the proceedings, to say nothing of the image thus projected.

Usually a Grand Officer will, if asked prior to the meeting, be pleased to present a Grand Lodge Certificate to a newly raised Brother. It is quite wrong as well as discourteous, for an announcement to be made that the Grand Officer will now present a Certificate and to note from the expression on his face that this is the very first time he has heard the subject mentioned.

All too frequently we hear the cry: 'why cannot more Grand Officers be appointed so that every Lodge has one of its own?' As with most things in life the scarcity of appointments to Grand Rank illustrates the value which should be attached to the appointment as well as to those who are so appointed.

Promotion within Grand Rank is not as rare as one might imagine. A brother holding Grand Rank for a number of years, usually upwards of seven can be promoted upon the recommendation of his Lodge if in London and if approved by the Grand Master and in Provinces and Districts upon the recommendation of his Provincial or District Grand Master and again approved by the Grand Master.

It must be stated clearly that such promotions are not automatic, nor indeed is a recommendation necessarily approved but they can and do occur each year as reference to the Masonic Year Book will clearly show.

One final point worth remembering yourself and passing on to the Master. If a Grand Officer should attend your lodge 'officially' the gavel should not be offered to him unless he is accompanied by his own Director of Ceremonies which will mean that he visits your lodge in his own right and by virtue of holding his own Patent. Such is the case in Provinces or Districts whereby the Provincial or District Grand Master, his Deputy or Assistants make regular visits to lodges within their own Province or District.

Needless to say should the Grand Master, the Pro Grand Master or the Deputy or Assistant Grand Master visit your lodge you will be 'fully instructed' on the precise details of your own participation and that of the Master of the Lodge.

Chapter Eight

The Visiting Grand Officer

THE TITLE of this chapter has of necessity to cover patterns of behaviour in London, the Provinces and in Districts Overseas.

In recent years in London a Visiting Grand Officer scheme has been introduced for facilitating visits to Lodges within the London area that do not have a Grand Officer as a member of the Lodge. In Provinces various systems are in operation whereby Grand Officers visit Lodges at Installation Meetings only or in some cases, only at meetings other than Installation Meetings. In Districts Overseas local custom and practice varies so widely for it to be impossible to formulate a composite picture of given behaviour.

The purpose of this Chapter is to explain the procedure to be adopted when news of a visiting Grand Officer is made known to the Lodge Secretary. Clearly the members of the Lodge will wish to show THEIR lodge in the best possible light to the Grand Officer concerned and this should commence with a nicely phrased letter of welcome from the Secretary in which he should tell the visitor something of the Lodge history, its progress and current standing.

The membership of the Lodge is of course an important feature of the news which should be imparted to the distinguished guest telling him of the trend factors on membership, attendance, charitable donations, together with any other important facts concerning the particular lodge. This is the time when any request to carry out any task in the lodge should be made. Do you want him to present a Grand Lodge Certificate? Do you wish him to close the V.S.L. at the conclusion of the meeting ? is there any other task you would like him to perform?

Finally, tell him in that letter that he will be met by Bro . . . on his arrival and, if appropriate, that car parking space will be provided for him, in which event, make very certain that space is reserved and clearly indicated. Then ensure that the Brother so designated is also appraised of what he has to do on the day. The Visiting Grand Officer should be brought directly to you as the Director of Ceremonies of the Lodge. It is you who should introduce him to the Master, Secretary and other senior brethren of the lodge in order that he can feel 'at home' as quickly as possible. Ensure that he is shown his seat in the Lodge, and then explain what you wish him to do if he is to participate, do not leave him wondering what will happen, make sure he knows in detail well in advance. If it is the custom in your lodge for a Visiting Grand Officer to be invited to close the V.S.L., escort him with a court bow both when collecting him and returning him to his seat.

Explain where he will be situated in the outgoing procession and when you reach that part of the ceremony do not attempt to take him by the hand rather give him a court bow from a short distance away and then precede him to the place you have already indicated in the procession, completing the act with another court bow.

If a Festive Board is to follow the meeting it is important that the Visiting Grand Officer meets as many of the members of the Lodge as possible. On this occasion it is permissible for guests to be left until last in the process of introduction. It is a picture of the lodge and its members that the Visiting Grand Officer wishes to formulate, and to report upon if required. You should therefore arrange prior to the meeting that the members of the Lodge will make themselves available for a short period in that phase which follows immediately after the meeting in order that this 'getting to know' procedure can be smoothly accomplished. Introduce each member yourself, explain who they are, what they do or have done in the Lodge in the past. This is particularly important for all too frequently older Past Masters can be overlooked which is very sad particularly if they have given years of service to the Craft.

Ensure the Visiting Grand Officer is supplied with some refreshment. If the bar space is restricted, arrangements should be made in advance so that drinks can be obtained for him without delay. When the appropriate time arrives escort him into the Dining Room either with the Master or prior to the Master whichever local custom demands. The Visiting Grand Officer will of course be asked to take wine with the Master and it is sometimes the local custom for him to be invited by the Master to take wine with the Brethren although this is not of course mandatory.

At the appropriate point in the toast list the Visiting Grand Officer will be called upon to respond either for Grand Lodge or on behalf of the Province of District depending upon which he is representing and at this time it is important that you as the Director of Ceremonies should make certain that he is properly announced with all his styles and titles, at the same time calling upon the brethren for their complete silence. A nice gesture is to stand behind the Visiting Grand Officer whilst he is speaking so that you can ensure he is correctly seated at the conclusion of his speech.

It is not considered correct etiquette for a Grand Officer visiting or otherwise to be asked to respond on behalf of the 'Guests'.

When the proceedings are at an end and the time has come for the Visiting Grand Officer to depart from the meeting it would be courteous for him to be escorted to his transport and thanked for attending the meeting. Such treatment of a Visiting Grand Officer will not only result in your lodge being well considered, but also being thought of as very well organised from the start to the finish.

Turning now to the visit of a Provincial or District Grand Master, a Deputy Provincial or District Grand Master or an Assistant Provincial or District Grand Master, they will in all normal cases be accompanied by their own Director of Ceremonies who will undoubtedly make contact with your Lodge and probably you as Director of Ceremonies to tell you what he requires organising prior to the visit taking place. In many cases such visit will be the subject of a printed procedure list on which will be formulated the precise format for the day. The Director of Ceremonies will first of all request admission for himself, then DEMAND admission for the person he is escorting, then call upon you and your Assistant Director of Ceremonies and your Deacons to form a procession to escort the Visiting Dignitary into the lodge. The Provincial or District Director of Ceremonies will give all the commands and in these circumstances your only duty is to follow carefully his instructions.

On this occasion much of the processional work of the lodge will come ander the control of the Provincial or District Director of Ceremonies and in particular the closing of the V.S.L. by the Visiting Dignitary and the subsequent outgoing procession will certainly be so controlled but in every case the 'who does what' procedure should be invoked for we really cannot have any mistakes on such an important visit can we.?

Similarly the entry to the Festive Board of the Master and the Visiting Dignitary will be controlled by the Provincial or District Director of Ceremonies and in all other respects the Festive Board will be controlled by him. It is not unusual for the Visiting Dignitary to leave the Festive Board after the Master has replied to his toast and this will be accomplished by the Provincial or District Director of Ceremonies calling the brethren to order whilst the Visiting Dignitary retires from the room. When this occurs it is a mark of respect if a small deputation of say two or three of the senior brethren also take the opportunity to leave the room temporarily to thank the Visiting Dignitary and his Director of Ceremonies for making the visit to the lodge. This action is always appreciated and completes in a happy manner the visit of a visiting V.I.P. Always make quite sure that the final departure of the V.I.P., is accomplished without the need to move cars around in a car park, in other words get it right at the start and it will be right at the finish, hence the 'reserved car parking space'.

Chapter Nine

Salutations

THE SUBJECT of Salutations probably causes as many headaches for Directors of Ceremonies as any other than can arise at a Lodge meeting. Let us therefore start with the usual Lodge meeting where we have Provincial or District Officers only to salute.

In most Provinces and Districts it is usually the case that the Officers of the Province or District are saluted with three followed by the Officers of other Provinces and Districts and Holders of Senior London Grand Rank and London Grand Rank. The senior officer in each case will reply, but it is essential to ascertain before the Lodge is opened, who that is and that he knows he will have to reply. A Holder of Senior London Grand Rank or London Grand Rank must NOT reply in a Provincial Lodge, equally a Provincial or District Grand Officer must NOT reply in a London Lodge.

Now to the subject of Grand Officers. Should the Lodge be honoured with a visit from a Grand Officer his name and rank should be established prior to the commencement of the meeting. He will of course be saluted with three before all other Officers present. If there is more than one Grand Officer in attendance then the senior officer present will reply and in so doing will thank the brethren on behalf of his brother Grand Officer(s) as well as himself.

We now move to the slightly more complicated business of a Very Worshipful Brother being in attendance who is of course entitled to a salutation of five, and who would normally, if he is the senior officer present and the only one of that rank be saluted on his own.

There are other occasions which provide skilfully laid Director of Ceremonies man traps for those who do not carry out the pre-meeting planning with the utmost care. For example any Past Deputy or Assistant Provincial or District Grand Master who has served five years in office in his own Province or District is entitled to receive a salutation of five after he has left office so be warned, check, check, and check again especially when you have a Grand Officer attending your meeting with whom you are not acquainted. He could well be the one who will cause you to lose your one hundred per cent record of proficiency in dealing with salutations in your lodge.

The *Book of Constitutions* (rule six) gives a complete list of salutations for the various ranks of Grand Officer and you should learn this list by heart in order that you can, at will, be sure of the command you should give even though you receive very short notice of the Grand Officer's arrival. If you are hesitant to rely on your memory in an emergency, carry a copy of the text in your wallet.

In the case of a Provincial or District Grand Master or his Deputy or Assistants attending a lodge they will certainly be accompanied by a Provincial or District Director of Ceremonies or Deputy or Assistant Grand Director of Ceremonies who will attend to the salutation for the dignitary he is accompanying.

In the very unlikely event that your Lodge will receive a visit from either the Grand Master, the Pro Grand Master or the Deputy or Assistant Grand Master, they also will always be accompanied by a Grand Director of Ceremonies who will, without any doubt at all, communicate with you well before the day of the event and instruct you in the ceremonial in which you will be involved and very probably have some form of rehearsal prior to the start of the meeting itself.

A question very often asked is exactly when should salutations be given in a private lodge. There is no set ruling on this matter, and it is for each lodge to determine the place in the meeting which suits the members. Many lodges take the salutations immediately after the Minutes have been read and signed. Others take the salutations on the risings. Some take them just prior to the risings being commenced. It is recommended that each lodge determines at its Lodge Committee meeting precisely when such salutations will be taken and then this should be adhered to in the future. As has been said already there is no rule in force so you should adopt the time honoured practice of pleasing the majority.

For the record, the following salutations are listed in the *Book of Constitutions* under rule Six:–

Most Worshipful Brethren Present and Past –	Eleven
Deputy & Assistant Grand Masters Present and Past –	Nine
Other Right Worshipful Brethren –	Seven
Very Worshipful Brethren –	Five
All other Grand Officers –	Three

Within their own Provinces of Districts present
Deputy and Assistant Provincial Grand Masters – Five.

Past Deputy and Assistant Provincial or District Grand Masters with five years service or more are also entitled to receive a salutation of five but ONLY in their own Province or District.

Other Provincial or District Grand Officers – Three.
In London – Holders of Senior London and
London Grand Rank – Three.
In Lodges abroad not under Districts,
Holders of Overseas Grand Rank – Three.

Chapter Ten

Training Others

THIS IS a most difficult area on which to advise.

Those who are extremely competent when enacting the ceremonies are not necessarily gifted in the same way in passing that ability to others. It takes a very skilful and dedicated brother to cater for all the requirements of the Lodge of Instruction for, as we all know, every member learns the ritual at his own pace and the clever Preceptor is the one who knows the pace of each of his charges and ensures that the slow do not hold back the more capable, whilst the speed of the more capable should never be allowed to dishearten the slower learner. That statement sounds rather obvious but it takes a very special person to arrange that every member of the Lodge of Instruction feels he is getting real help and encouragement as well as seeing progress in his own performance.

So how do we produce this desirable paragon of virtue and competency? Perhaps the best way to establish a code of learning for each and every member of the lodge is to give them an identical format when they first attend the Lodge of Instruction in other words a list of ideal achievements. These must of necessity result in a gradual and ongoing series of learning over a period of years leading from office to office so that each brother gains the maximum advantage from his year in the chair.

In an ideal world the new member should be allowed to attend for a number of weeks, possibly even a few months, at the Lodge of Instruction and certainly until he has become familiar with all the brethren who regularly attend and has seen for himself, and established for himself, the simple fact that this is the place where everyone comes to learn and that those same people are fallible, human and make mistakes at times, albeit over a period they do progress.

When the 'new boy' has thus started to feel comfortable in the company of others then this is the time to start him on his way with an individualised learning programme. Setting targets for him to achieve and watching closely his progress or lack of progress, allows the skilled Preceptor to rein back or push a little harder according to the ability and enthusiasm of the member.

We must all remember those school days when some subjects came easily to us whilst others seemed to be so far beyond our comprehension, indeed the teacher could have been from another planet. Those same abilities or lack of them apply to every candidate we take into the Craft.

Do remember that your knowledge, which has undoubtedly been gained through many years of personal experience, cannot be transmitted to a 'new boy' in a few short months. Also bear in mind that if the same 'new boy' does not progress by learning at the same speed as Brother 'X' then he is obviously going to feel a failure and is going to believe that he will never achieve the chair of King Solomon.

We are all highly different individuals, we all learn at different speeds, a clever Preceptor will use that knowledge to his advantage. Setting a small target is far better than a large multi-page unit which is so daunting that it creates in a candidate who is short of confidence the belief that he will never be able to learn all the ritual so he may as well stop coming to the Lodge of Instruction now, for clearly it is not for people like him.

We wonder how many new members to the Craft have been discouraged in the manner suggested. Learn a little, feel proud, and then tackle another paragraph or so, that is the way to learn for it also establishes confidence and shows results in the process.

So what have we covered and established in this chapter?

Firstly, that we should set a new candidate an annual target at which to aim. Secondly, that we should break down the target into easily manageable parts and, in such a way that they become targets, week upon week, and month upon month. A little and often is the answer. If you need an ongoing example of the way a candidate feels after his first exposure to the ritual at a Lodge of Instruction try to remember your own reaction when you were told that everything that happened to you on the night of your Initiation was learned by heart and repeated from memory. You just could not believe it could you? Well, that is how he feels too!

For the assistance of Preceptors a chart is given at the end of this book which illustrates the manner in which an annual plan can be put together for the benefit of all the members of the Lodge of Instruction.

Chapter Eleven

Correcting Faults

THIS CHAPTER may sound at first reading as though it should be dealt with under the heading 'Training Others' but this is not necessarily so. We are to deal here with those habits which are developed by brethren who are not necessarily in the first flush of youth and who have perhaps become accustomed to a certain way of carrying out a task in another lodge which is not in conformity with either the ritual you work or the meaning of the masonic inference which is behind the particular degree being worked.

To say that tact and diplomacy are required in ample abundance is perhaps a gross understatement, for there is a very wide gulf between correcting a young enthusiastic master mason who is struggling to reach peak performance and a seasoned veteran of many years standing perhaps even one who has attained Provincial or District Grand Rank.

How then do we approach this problem? The first point to make is that you must enlist the help of the brother who has this particular fault by explaining to him that you are having a difficult problem perhaps at the Lodge of Instruction in which you feel he can be of considerable assistance.

The problem you will explain is that certain brethren insist on carrying out this particular part of the ceremony in this way (then describe the problem he has in as graphic terms as possible) whereas you will say as you know the correct way to carry out this part of the ceremony is by . . .!

This is one and only one way of gaining assistance and at the same time correcting a fault.

There are more direct methods but the easiest to use is ALWAYS to get the brother whose fault you are seeking to correct sitting metophorically on your side of the desk looking at the problem with you, rather than having a confrontation from which strained relations undoubtedly will result. In every case the 'please help me to help them' approach will work and will not offend. Try it – it really does work, that is a promise.

Chapter Twelve

Why Bother?

THIS MAY be an appropriate time to ask the question: 'Why bother'?

After all it is not your problem is it? If the Junior Deacon has not learnt his part properly and does not know how to carry out the ceremony of Initiation, or if the Master is not sure who exactly is going to prompt him if he needs help, or indeed if a Grand Officer arrives unannounced and cannot find his own seat, why do you have to bother?

We would imagine that your reaction to the previous paragraph is one of absolute horror, but why? Could it be that the answer is manifold pride, pride in your lodge, pride in your reputation as a well organised Director of Ceremonies, and pride in the way in which your lodge treats its visiting brethren. If the answer is YES, and we are sure that it is, then that pride must extend to all areas of the lodge operation, from the accurate printing of the Lodge Summons to the conclusion of the Tyler's toast. It is quite true to say that the few care for the many in Freemasonry and it is probably also true to say that it is only when the total content of the planning and organisation of a lodge meeting is understood and appreciated that the work of the Director of Ceremonies together with that of Brother Secretary are fully recognised.

'If a job is worth doing, it is worth doing well', is an old saying but nevertheless absolutely true.

Chapter Thirteen

Training the Master Elect

THIS SECTION is far more important than the reader will appreciate at first view. The normal view of the training of the Master begins and ends with his being adjudged to be proficient in the performance of the three degrees of Craft masonry and his ability to know in brief form the basic rules and regulations by which the lodge should be operated. Any further requirement of knowledge in depth can usually be left to the Secretary of the lodge who is of course the 'Merlin of the Court' He can and will answer all difficult questions so the need for the Master to know more than a few basic and recurring points of procedure is unnecessary. After all he is there for only one year, is he not?

How wrong can he be!

On taking his Obligation the Master Elect affirms in open lodge that he is 'able and willing to undertake the management of the lodge, well skilled in the Ancient Charges, Regulations and Landmarks of the Order'. The Installing Master then continues 'Can you, my worthy Brother conscientiously undertake the Mastership of this Lodge under those qualifications'?

The Master Elect then replies 'I can'.

Have you ever stopped to think that probably only one Master Elect in a hundred can and does answer that question accurately? You will notice we have not used the expression honestly for we are sure that the majority do feel they are so qualified, but, and it is a very big but, supposing that every Master Elect had to sit an examination paper and achieve at least a 70% mark before being allowed to take that Obligation, how many would pass? We dread to think!

Whose fault is this one may ask? The answer is the Lodge, and more particularly its Past Masters who have failed to put in place a proper training plan for those who are coming through to the Master's Chair.

We have all witnessed the Brother who arrives at a Festive Board after possibly fifteen years in the Lodge and is confronted by the Official Toast List and views it as though it is a set of instructions written in Chinese, having not a clue as to the correct pronunciation of the names or the content of the list itself, or for that matter who does what and when.

We have now arrived at the point of this Chapter, the training of the Master Elect.

The Master Elect of the Lodge, upon subsequent Installation, is in charge from that precise moment and this is most decidedly not the time to start to learn the duties and indeed the responsibilities of his office.

When and how then should this training, for such it must be, begin in earnest so that the Brother aspiring to do everything correctly during his year will feel comfortable, competent, and fully briefed for the year of Mastership that lies ahead and equally to the point, to be able to ensure that his successor in office is also as well briefed as he is himself?

The Preceptor of the Lodge of Instruction and the Director of Ceremonies can and will be towers of strength in such matters. It is therefore essential that time is allocated for the Master Elect to learn those extra duties which he is called upon to perform in addition to the carrying through of the Ceremonies.

It is an excellent plan for the Master Elect to be taken through the Festive Board Proceedings from start to finish commencing with the list of those with whom he wishes to take wine. Caution an over enthusiastic Master Elect from extending this list beyond four or five, for the object is to include everyone but not to interrupt what should be the opportunity for the brethren to indulge in social intercourse.

The Master must ensure that the after proceedings are conducted with decorum and, in particular, that silence is obtained immediately he sounds his gavel.

To keep interrupting the brethren and thereby stopping them from enjoying their conversation is to be discouraged for it has a distinctly umdesirable effect upon the evening. An ideal list is given hereunder:–

1. The Master with everyone.
2. The Master with Grand Officers.
3. The Master with the Initiate (if appropriate).
4. The Master with the Guests.
5. The Master with the Past Masters & Officers of the Lodge.
6. The Master with the Master Elect. (Election night only).

These takings of wine should be fitted into the proceedings in such a manner that the brethren will not be interrupted during the eating of a particular course. It is quite possible for the total of five or six wine takings to be accomplished between the first and second course so that the proceedings are not interrupted again and the brethren thereby enjoy their Festive Board to the full.

Moving now to the Toast List, it is very important indeed that the Master Elect is taken through this list a number of times prior to the night of his Installation. No Master should meet the Toast List for the very first time when taking his seat at the Festive Board on the night of his Installation. Ensure that he not only reads out aloud the names and ranks of the Brethren but fully understands the groupings into which they fall. Ensure that he realises it not necessary for the military and civil decorations of Grand Officers to be stated and that he also fully understands 'masonic fire' if such is given in your Lodge.

On the subject of masonic fire, this should be given with total decorum and the Director of Ceremonies has a duty to ensure that such masonic fire is never speeded up to the point whereby the senior and perhaps older brethren are not only unable to participate but also become annoyed with the younger members for their apparent disrespect for the Craft and the Lodge.

To say it never happens is untrue but when it does it is the clear duty of the Director of Ceremonies and the Master to ensure it is not repeated.

The Master has a further duty to ensure that the Festive Board is conducted with a clear timetable in mind. The brethren have a right to expect that time is not wasted and that the proceedings will be carried through with the minimum of time consuming activities, so that those who have trains to catch are not forced to leave before the proceedings are ended.

The ideal length of speeches, when given, is three to five minutes, longer than that and the brethren are frequently tempted to talk to each other and the courtesy of the occasion is lost.

On occasions of particular merit the meeting may well be enhanced by the visit of the Provincial or District Grand Master, his Deputy or one of his Assistants. When this occurs the visiting Officer will usually be accompanied by a Provincial or District Grand Director of Ceremonies who will take charge of the proceedings ceremonially speaking, and this will usually include a large part of the Festive Board.

Such Director of Ceremonies will of course introduce the Officer he has brought and it is normal for the Master of the Lodge to have a SHORT speech of welcome on such an occasion, rather than the stark announcement that: 'We will now, drink a toast to' without any speech of welcome being given. It assists considerably in the projection of the Lodge image for the visiting officer to see that the Master himself has taken the time and trouble to prepare his work for the Festive Board with care and consideration for his guests, high and low ranking alike.

Chapter Fourteen

The Installation Meeting

THIS IS the one meeting of the year when the Director of Ceremonies must of necessity be very much in evidence for this is the meeting at which he demonstrates to the Lodge the manner in which he controls every aspect of the Lodge ceremonial.

The success or failure of the Installation Meeting in terms of satisfaction for the members and guests lies in the planning, rehearsing, and organisation which precede it by many weeks, and probably by many months.

Clearly the Master has to be rehearsed and taken through the pre-installation part of the meeting then through the Obligating and Entrusting of his successor. The Inner Working is of course, learnt by the majority of Masters to be used by them only once in their masonic life. It is therefore most important for the Installing Master that he carries out this highly personal ceremony in the most proficient, dedicated and caring manner possible.

The general tone of the Installation Meeting is set by the Director of Ceremonies and *ALL* will look to him, probably more than at any other meeting, for help, advice, and general guidance in virtually every aspect of the ceremony. It is therefore vital that the Director of Ceremonies keeps a very cool, calm and controlled demeanour throughout the entire meeting, for if he loses, or even looks as though he is losing total control then the day is spoilt not only for the Master but also the Master Elect and all who are present.

Let us then move through the Installation Meeting from the start of the incoming procession right through to the outgoing procession and the conclusion of the meeting.

First we shall arrive earlier than usual for clearly at this important meeting the brethren will all be arriving earlier than usually they do at a regular meeting. You will want to go through your check list in a calm and orderly manner well in advance of anyone requiring your advice or assistance.

Let us then accept that you have completed your check of the Lodge room and are satisfied that every item that will be needed is in place and ready for use. Did you remember the Collar Horse for the Officers Collars? Have you made quite certain that you have put reserved notices on the seats required for those taking part in the ceremony?

Have you reserved a seat for the Provincial or District Grand Master's representative? Do you know his name and rank? You should have checked this well before the day of the meeting. Has a car parking place been reserved for the representative and has he been advised? Has someone been detailed to meet him and ensure he is properly cared for as soon as he arrives? Has the brother so detailed been instructed to bring the representative directly to you in order that you can show him his seat as well as discuss the various points of the meeting in which he might be involved, such as giving an address or closing the V.S.L. at the end of the meeting or perhaps even presenting a Grand Lodge Certificate during the course of the meeting?

Are we to present to the Installing Master a Past Masters' Collar and Collar Jewel and a Past Master's Breast Jewel? If the answer is 'Yes' then have they been placed in a convenient position for the newly Installed Master to present at the appropriate time in the ceremony? Has a glass of water been arranged ready for the Installing Master's use? Have the Past Masters who will occupy the Wardens' and Inner Guard's chairs during the Installation been rehearsed in their duties? If not why was this not done some time ago and certainly before today?

Assuming that this has been organised correctly have we a complete list of those brethren who are to participate, particularly in the explanation of the three sets of working tools and the three addresses at the end of the meeting?

We have now started the meeting, the opening ode has been sung the Master has opened the Lodge in the first degree and the Minutes have been read and signed. The Master will now wish to thank all his Officers, which may be achieved in a variety of ways but the one usually adopted in private lodges is for the Master to ask all his Officers to line up in the North East in order of seniority so that he may thank them for their assistance during his year as Master.

Now you start work, for the task of ensuring they do in fact line up in the correct order is your responsibility. When you are satisfied that the order is correct you then instruct the Senior Warden to move in front of the Master who will in all probability shake his hand. It is usual in many lodges for the Collar of office of the brother who has just shaken hands with the Master to be taken from him at this stage in order that it may be placed on the Collar Horse.

It should be noted here that every Officer retains his office in the Lodge until a new officer is appointed by the incoming Master. It is therefore perfectly permissible for all the Officers to retain their collars until the Director of Ceremonies or Assistant Director of Ceremonies comes to collect the collar when a new appointment to that office is announced by the newly Installed Master.

We have now arrived at the point where the Master will ask the three designated Past Masters to accept his offer to assist him in the next part of the ceremony. The request having been acknowledged you should approach the brother concerned, giving him a court bow (moving the head only) take him by the hand and deliver him to the position ascribed to him, completing the action with another court bow. Remove the Senior Warden (if he is to be the next Master) to a previously reserved seat as near as possible to yourself primarily for your own convenience later in the ceremony. Carry out this same task with the Junior Warden and the Inner Guard.

We are now ready to move to the Second Degree which the Master should proceed to do after having asked all Entered Apprentices to retire for a short time.

Having opened the lodge in the second degree we now start the first part of the Installation Ceremony proper by rising, approaching the Master Elect giving him a court bow, taking him by the hand and moving to the centre of the lodge, saluting the Master in the second degree and then presenting the Master Elect in the usual form.

The Master will then thank you, and you should return to your seat, the preamble having been completed. The Master Elect, having signified his acceptance of, and adherence to the Ancient

Charges and Regulations he then removes his gloves and advances to the pedestal and takes his Obligation, repeating the words of the Master. Have you established who, if necessary will prompt the Master?

The Obligation having been completed and the Master having raised the Master Elect you should advance and return him to his seat completing the action with a court bow.If your working differs from this practice please amend this instruction to suit your own requirements.

Fellowcrafts are now asked to retire for a short time and the Lodge is opened in the third degree after which all Master Masons are asked to retire.

The Board of Installed Masters having been formed and the Master having been Obligated and Installed into the chair of King Solomon, the Provincial or District Grand Master or his representative will then wish to congratulate the newly Installed Master. You *MUST* ensure that he does so *FIRST* and before any other over enthusiastic brother does so. This action not only shows the good organisation of the Lodge and that the correct way things should be done is understood, but is also the correct protocol to observe.

Frequently all the brethren will then wish to give their own personal congratulations to the newly installed Master and when this is completed the lodge is frequently called off and tea is taken. If this is the case in your Lodge you must ensure that the Master accompanies the Provincial or District Grand Master's representative from the Temple before anyone else. You must also ensure that the break is as short as possible.

Let us assume that tea, if taken, is completed and that the Past Masters have re-assembled in the Temple and the Lodge has been called on. We now have to admit the Master Masons, making sure that the designated brethren who will form the procession are left until last. Lodge practices vary and it is difficult if not impossible to legislate for all forms of processions. Many lodges have every available Master Mason in the procession, others have seven, many have just four with the Director of Ceremonies making the fifth.

Assuming local custom and practice have been observed and that the three perambulations and the requisite salutations have been completed we then move to the presentation of the Warrant of the Lodge, the *Book of Constitutions* (please see that it is the latest copy available – completely updated) and the By-Laws of the Lodge after which the Installing Master says to the Master 'You will will now appoint and invest your Officers'.

At this point the Director of Ceremonies starts to work his way through the role of Officers, having learned by heart the correct order well before the meeting. A system to be recommended that will ease this part of the ceremony for the Director of Ceremonies is for the Assistant Director of Ceremonies to collect the various items for presentation and leave the Director of Ceremonies to present and deal with the Brother who is being appointed or who has been elected to a given office. A good partnership worked out well in advance not only looks smart to the assembled brethren but it saves considerable time and maintains a desirable progression throughout the entire ceremony.

It should be remembered at this point that the Organist should not be presented unless he is a member of the Lodge. It is perfectly permissible for an Honorary Organist to be taken to the Master at the conclusion of the Investiture of Officers to receive a handshake from the Master and the thanks of the Lodge for his work through-out the year but he must NOT be invested with a collar of office.

The Stewards having been invested and advised of their duties by the Master should be taken to their places and seated 'en bloc'. It should be noted that although many lodges continue to show on their summons a rank of Senior Steward there is in fact no such rank listed in the *Book of Constitutions*. Any reference to such a rank should be removed and certainly the Director of Ceremonies when asking the newly Installed Master whom he appoints to certain offices should NEVER say 'whom do you appoint Senior Steward'. Equally Brother Secretary should resist any attempt to elevate a brother in print, be he a Past Master or not.

The Master having been advised that Bro . . . having been elected Tyler of the Lodge, he is now presented after the Inner Guard has taken his post outside the door of the Lodge. After being invested with his Collar and having had the Sword returned to him he is taken to the West where he salutes the Master and returns to his post outside the door thus allowing the Inner Guard to resume his correct place inside the door of the Lodge.

The Addresses then follow with each Brother being escorted to the point of his address and returned to his seat afterwards. At this point the Director of Ceremonies should announce 'Worshipful Master that completes the ceremony of your Installation. Will you now be pleased to continue with the remaining business of the Lodge?'

Do remember to give a court bow to each Officer Designate as you collect him and likewise when you release him after arriving at his new post in the lodge. A court bow is a courteous way of acknowledging the start and finish of an action in connection with another person without the necessity for words.

The remaining business having been accomplished the meeting then follows the normal format except that a Provincial or District representative should be placed in the correct position in the outgoing procession.

The following ceremonial may be used when Installing a Past Master in the Chair of King Solomon

DC presents the Master Elect in the usual manner to which the Master replies . . . *Your presentation* etc. etc. etc . . .

Master then gives the preamble through to the words '*Mastership of this lodge on these qualifications*'.

Master Elect says '*I can*'.

The Installing Master then says '*At your Installation on a previous occasion you signified your assent to the Ancient Charges and Regulations of our order, do you now confirm your adherence to, and support of them*?

Master Elect says '*I do*'.

The Installing Master then says '*You will advance to the pedestal and recite your Obligation as Master of the Lodge. Kneel on your right knee, place your right hand on the V.S.L.*'

Master Elect then recites his Obligation.

D.C., takes Master Elect back to his seat.

Master instructs all FC's to retire.

Lodge is opened in the third degree.

Master instructs Master Masons to retire.

Master then declares the Board of Installed Masters' open.

DC, places the Master Elect immediately in front of the pedestal and instructs him to kneel.

After the prayer has been given the Installing Master says 'At your Installation on a previous occasion you took the solemn Obligation of an Installed Master, that remains binding upon you so long as you shall live, you will however re-affirm that Obligation by sealing it with your lips three times on the V.S.L.'.

Installing Master then gives the explanation of the three great lights in Freemasonry and raises the Master Elect and places him in the South East.

Master Elect then says '*On a previous occasion the words signs and grip of an Installed Master were communicated to you and you wear the badge of that office.*

I now invest you with the collar and jewel of that office which is the square that being the highest honour the lodge can bestow on any of its members' . . . then continues with the explanation of the square through to the end.

The Master Elect is then taken in the usual manner and placed in the chair of King Solomon.

The Installing Master then presents the WM, with his gavel together with the usual words of explanation after which he (the Installing Master) instructs the brethren to salute the newly Installed Master five times after which he requests the newly Installed Master to invest 'THE' Immediate Past Master.

The Board of Installed Masters is then closed by the W.M. The PGM or his representative will then congratulate the newly Installed Master.

MM's are then admitted and the rest of the ceremony follows the usual Ritual working.

Following the third declaration from the South and after the newly Installed Master has been saluted three times with the EA salute, the Installing Master should return to the pedestal and instruct the brethren to be seated after he has said '*the working tools of an E.A. are --- but I shall NOT take up your time or that of the Lodge by explaining them at length*'.

The Installing Master then presents to the Master the Warrant, the *Book of Constitutions*, and the By-laws of the Lodge.

The Installing Master then says '*You will now appoint and invest your officers*'.

The following ceremonial should be used when the Master of the Lodge is to continue in office for a second year

Very occasionally the circumstances require that a Master continue in office for a second year. This often presents the inexperienced Director of Ceremonies with a real problem usually because such a situation has never occurred in his lodge previously. The answer to this situation is indeed very simple as will be quickly appreciated.

When the appropriate item is reached on the agenda the Director of Ceremonies should rise from his seat and standing in the South East make the following statement:

> Brethren W.Bro . . . having been elected for a second year in office I now proclaim him Worshipful Master of the . . . (state name and number) lodge and I now call upon you to salute him as EA Freemasons' five times taking the time from me.

When this has been completed and the Brethren are told to be seated the Director of Ceremonies then moves to the investiture of Officers without further instruction and says '*Worshipful Master whom do you appoint as Senior Warden of the Lodge*'. He then moves through the list of Officers and completes the meeting in the usual way.

It is quite unnecessary for the address to the Master to be given on this occasion. This also applies to the Wardens if they also are to continue in office for a second year. The address to the Brethren should always be given.

The Director of Ceremonies should remember that this procedure will result in a very short meeting since none of the usual perambulations, salutations, or opening in any degree other than the first will take place. The Secretary and Director of Ceremonies will require to plan the timing of such a meeting very carefully for the ceremonial described above will take only twenty to twenty five minutes at most.

Chapter Fifteen

The Festive Board

THE ARRANGEMENTS for the seating at the Festive Board are frequently undertaken by the Stewards of the Lodge. This however does not in any way mean that the Director of Ceremonies has no part to play or no responsibility for seeing that the work has been carried out both efficiently and correctly.

As will be realised, any Grand Officer should be seated on the right of the Master, if two Grand Officers are present they should be seated according to rank. If it should be found that they rank equally the position of their seating will be determined by the Secretary who will advise you of the year of their appointments. Yes we knew you would ask: 'What if they were appointed in the same year?' We believe the correct answer is that they should be seated in alphabetical order since that is the way in which they will have been invested in Grand Lodge.

Assuming that all is well with the seating and that protocol has been observed, let us not forget that in many Lodges it is the custom for an Initiate to be seated on the right of the Master no matter what the rank of the Grand Officer in attendance.

The Director of Ceremonies announces the entry of the Master to the Festive Board and the Master or the Lodge Chaplain says Grace.

It should be noted here that ONLY the Master should use the gavel at the Festive or Social Board. It is the DUTY of the Director of Ceremonies to ensure that the gavel is respected immediately.

The taking of wine has already been dealt with in the previous Chapter so it is unnecessary to repeat it here.

The meal being completed and the waiters and waitresses having left the room the first duty of the Director of Ceremonies is to ensure that if Grace is to be sung in your Lodge then the Lodge Organist or Pianist is ready to play.

It is quite unnecessary for the waiters or waitresses to be excluded if masonic fire is not to be given.

The first of the 'Official Toasts' of the evening is of course to The Queen and the Craft, it has been clearly laid down by Grand Lodge that where the National Anthem is sung at the Festive Board this should be done prior to the toast being drunk and the masonic fire given.

It should be clearly stated here that this Official Toast list is a continuous series of toasts, and long gaps between each toast are to be avoided, for not only does this delay the departure of guests it is also inconsiderate for those who may well have long journeys to make to return to their homes.

The second toast of the evening is to the Grand Master (currently) His Royal Highness the Duke of Kent.

Smoking may now be permitted.

The next is to the Pro Grand Master by name, the Deputy Grand Master by name, the Assistant Grand Master by name and the Grand Officers present and past.

Please note here that the term Grand *Lodge* Officers is totally wrong and should be corrected should it ever occur in your lodge, the correct terminology being Grand Officers.

You may perhaps have a Grand Officer present, and as a matter of courtesy you might ask him to respond. He may or he may not wish to do so in which case so be it. Should there be more than one Grand Officer present then the senior officer should always be asked first and if he declines he may suggest that the next most senior officer is asked.

The toast to the Provincial or District Grand Master is then taken.

The toast to the Deputy and Assistant Provincial or District Grand Masters and the Officers of Provincial or District Grand Lodge then follows.

The toast to the Master comes next and is usually given by the Immediate Past Master. There is absolutely no reason at all why this toast has to be of any great length, a simple toast with perhaps a mention of the work of the meeting and the control of the Master is all that is required. The response by the Master should give him the opportunity to make such announcements as he feels so inclined, as well as responding to the kind words said by the Immediate Past Master. In some Lodges it is the practice for this toast to be proposed only at Installation meetings.

We next move to the speech to the Initiate which should be given by a senior member of the Lodge preferably by a Past Master for such is the importance of the occasion that we should aim to impress upon the candidate the store which we set by the introduction of a new member into our lodge.

The reply by the Initiate should of course cover the thanks due to his Proposer and Seconder and to the members of the Lodge for accepting him into Freemasonry.

It is perfectly acceptable for the candidate to be advised prior to the meeting that he will be required to say a few words on the occasion of his Initiation and also to be told that he should commence his speech with the preamble 'Worshipful Master, Brother Wardens and Brethren'. It is, as we all know, completely unnecessary for him to endeavour to encompass every rank and title in masonic heirachy before saying his 'few words'. It should be impressed upon him quite clearly that everyone whom he meets that evening will have been through the same ceremony and is aware of the feelings which a Candidate experiences on the night of his Initiation.

The toast to the guests which follows is an opportunity for the Master to give one of his newer members the chance to 'say a few words in front of his fellow brethren.' It is of course quite surprising how many try to decline this request.

This is an opportunity for the Director of Ceremonies to speak to the brother so requested and try to instil in him a sense of confidence for his first speech at the Festive Board. it is the precursor of the many tasks he will have to perform, as well as speaking in front of his fellow brethren in the lodge, if he is to progress through to the chair of King Solomon.

It is therefore essential that the Master makes such requests to his younger members prior to the meeting itself to enable them to have the necessary time to prepare for the task they have been set.

In many Lodges the next toast, to which there may or may not be a reply, is of course to the Past Masters' and Officers of the Lodge. Again this is a golden opportunity for some younger brother to be given his chance to say a few words, the same comments as above apply here.

Finally the Tyler's toast.

In some lodges at an appropriate point in the toast list it has become customary for the brethren to drink a toast to 'Absent Brethren'. This is perfectly in order provided that it is not taken before the toast to the Queen and the Craft and until after the toast to the Grand Master. It should never be called the Nine o'clock toast, its correct title is the toast to Absent Brethren.

So called Silent Fire is to be deprecated and has no place in our Festive or Social Board proceedings.

There are occasions particularly at Installation Meetings when a singer is invited to render the Master's song and perhaps provide a little entertainment for the Brethren. It is the duty and responsibility of the Director of Ceremonies to ensure that the timing of such entertainment is in keeping with the overall Festive Board and that brethren are not inconvenienced by a lengthy performance no matter how entertaining the artist or artists may be.

Chapter Sixteen

Visiting Brethren

UNQUESTIONABLY EVERY lodge is proud to receive Visiting Brethren and equally unquestionably Visiting Brethren gain much from the visiting in which they partake. Friendships are renewed, new friends are found, and so the progress of our order thrives and grows. Each member of a Lodge will wish to invite Visiting Brethren to his Lodge for some special occasion, so how should we treat those who may never have been to our Lodge before?

It is the duty of the Junior Warden, so we are instructed, to ensure that every visitor to the Lodge is properly introduced and that he is entitled to enter the lodge room and be present whilst the ceremonies take place. Normally of course his host will go through the correct procedure and bring his guest to the Junior Warden and say 'This is Brother . . . my guest this evening, may I please introduce him to you?' or some other similar method of making the Junior Warden aware that a guest unknown to him is present.

What happens when that same guest arrives and his host is not present? Do all the brethren stand around and stare at the newcomer who is not known, making him feel extremely uncomfortable, or have you as Director of Ceremonies a system in place for dealing with that situation?

In the author's own Lodge it has been the custom for over sixty years for any visitor, once he steps inside the door, to be received by the Lodge Stewards who will immediately make sure he is looked after until his host arrives and is introduced to the Master and Wardens of the Lodge. Lesson one: the visitor is made to feel welcome.

First impressions are very important, you form instant and lasting mental pictures of the reception you received when you arrived at the Lodge of a friend. Whatever arrangements you have in your Lodge at this time, remember that the spirit of our order is one of brotherly love, care and concern. The Director of Ceremonies can do much to arrange that the Stewards are on duty from the start of the meeting even to the point of insisting that they are present at least forty-five minutes prior to the time of starting. This is first class training for your Stewards and a meaningful lesson in the overall care of visiting brethren, starting in their own lodge.

Let your Stewards tell their friends how their Lodge looks after visitors. It is quite amazing how such things are transmitted from one Lodge to another.

Lesson two: your Lodge image is enhanced.

There are odd occasions when a Director of Ceremonies might find he is faced with an occurrence outside his field of past experience. Such might well be the case of a visitor arriving at the lodge wearing what to the normal member might be regarded as strange regalia.

Such a brother might have been invited by someone in the Lodge who can vouch for him and will know of the Constitution to which he belongs and explain accordingly. However, what if a visitor should arrive with a letter from the United Grand Lodge of England saying he is a visitor from overseas who wishes to attend a meeting? He is known to no one in the lodge and if it were not for the letter he carries, could or could not be a member of the Craft.

Clearly this is a job for the Director of Ceremonies and the Junior Warden. The brother should obviously be proved in the degrees in which the lodge will be opened during the meeting.

Steps and signs vary in lodges. In some continental lodges the signs, grips and words of the first and second degrees are in the reverse order to ours.

The Junior Warden should then advise the Master that all is well and Brother Secretary can read the letter from Grand Lodge introducing the brother concerned. It is a nice gesture for such a visitor to be conducted to the East to enable the Master to greet him personally.

The ruling on regalia is quite clear, any brother who is a member of a lodge working under the auspices of the United Grand Lodge of England must wear English Constitution regalia when attending a lodge which is registered in the books of the United Grand Lodge of England.

A brother visiting from overseas or from the Scottish or Irish

Constitutions who is NOT a member of an English Constitution Lodge may wear his own particular regalia in an English Lodge.

If however at a later stage he should become a member of an English Lodge he must in addition to making a Declaration in open lodge (rule 163 f) also then wear English regalia in that Lodge and when he visits any lodge under the Constitution of the United Grand Lodge of England.

Visiting Brethren should be cherished. Their first visit to your lodge and its working still do much to influence their impression. Is yours a lodge which cares? Or a lodge which is insular? The members of which care only for themselves and disregard the happiness and satisfaction of the Visiting Brethren. Remember not everyone sees your lodge the way you see it!

Chapter Seventeen

The Initiate

THE DIRECTOR of Ceremonies can play a very big part indeed in the care, control and well-being of the Initiate on the night of his Initiation but let us stop at this point and go back in time to the point where a brother advises the Secretary that he has a Candidate for interview and please could he have a form to complete.

This can and should be a very good time for the Director of Ceremonies to ask a few questions of the prospective Proposer. How long has he known the Candidate, really known him? Has he for instance been to his home? Has he met his wife? His family? What is his profession or trade? Does he appreciate just what Freemasonry is expecting from him? What does he expect from Freemasonry? Does he appreciate the financial aspects of his membership? Has his wife been fully advised of such things? Is he known in the locality? Does he live or work within the locality or has an enquiry to be made under rule 158 *Book of Constitutions*.

These questions and many many more are fairly standard points which are raised for every new Candidate but they need asking before a form is completed not afterwards.

Newly Initiated members of the Craft are occasionally so thrilled by their own experience that they rush to bring into the Craft, friends of many years. Caution is to be recommended to temper the enthusiasm of such newly initiated brethren.

A good and caring Director of Ceremonies, can assist a well meaning Proposer, particularly when that same Proposer is a member of fairly short duration, by taking him on one side and asking if he can help the Proposer with his prospective Candidate. Can the Proposer perhaps bring him along after a Lodge of Instruction Meeting one evening in order that a number of the brethren particularly the Past Masters can have the opportunity of meeting him. Who is to second the Candidate?

This style of care and concern augers well with the general overall management approach of the Director of Ceremonies to the care and well-being of the Lodge.

We hear all too often of Candidates who are not seen after they have taken their Third Degree. There are no bad Candidates, there are certainly well meaning Proposers and Seconders who have not thought the whole process through from beginning to end. The Proposer and Seconder of a Candidate into Freemasonry undertake a lifetime of responsibility – it should never be forgotten!

It is to be recommended that the Director of Ceremonies spends a little time with the Candidate after he has taken his Third Degree to explain to him in some detail the meaning and symbolical interpretation of the ceremonies through which he has been conducted. He should follow this with a brief explanation of what is now required of him on his journey to the Master's chair.

It may sound trite to say so, but large numbers are not always either desirable or indeed necessary, quality not quantity is the answer. We have a great duty to every Candidate who enters our order both in caring for his enthusiasm, and ensuring that he receives proper instruction. Newly-made Brethren are influenced by virtually everything they hear, see and are told, so be there ready and willing to foster, nurture, and care for these new blooms for that is what they are. Their first few years in the Craft can and frequently do fashion their opinions for the rest of their masonic careers.

Do make certain that the candidate is fully informed about his dress on the day of his Initiation, and that he will be required to be prepared for that occasion. He should also be instructed in the procedure at the social board which follows. Entered Apprentices and Fellowcrafts must NOT wear gloves when being passed or raised, though they may do so at other meetings.

The Initiate should be seated on the right of the Senior Deacon on the night of his Initiation. It should also be remembered that the Initiate has no right to be included in the outgoing procession or to be seated on the right of the Worshipful Master at the social board. Although the latter act is customary in many lodges it is a courtesy not a right.

Finally it should be remembered that the Registration Form MUST be read before the ballot is taken and that the Master's declaration MUST be read in full.

Chapter Eighteen

The Warrant of the Lodge

THIS MAY seem at first glance a strange chapter to include in a book aimed at Directors of Ceremonies but it is most important that the information contained herein is understood and applied by all who have the overall care and concern of the lodge as their primary undertaking.

We all know that when a lodge is consecrated, the Consecrating Officer presents to the first Master the Warrant of the Lodge charging him to pass it to his successor when his year as Master is over. The Master of a Lodge when installing his successor uses such phrases as 'I now pass into your care the Warrant of the Lodge. For many years it has been in the hands of worthy and distinguished brethren and in entrusting it into your care I know that it will lose none of its lustre but will be passed to your successor pure and unsullied as you now receive it'.

Why then is the Warrant so important and why is the Master so frequently seen to be carrying it into the Lodge and why is he often seen to display it either before or immediately after the start of the Lodge meeting?

The answer can be found in rule 101 of the *Book of Constitutions* and it will no doubt come as a great shock to the reader to find that the Warrant does not 'belong' to the Lodge the Master in fact holds the Warrant in safe custody on behalf of the Grand Master. The Master (the rule continues) shall produce it at every meeting of the Lodge. Hence we can at once appreciate that a meeting at which the Warrant is not available is unconstitutional and cannot be held.

The Master of the Lodge is perhaps completely unaware for the entire period of his Mastership that he is holding the Warrant in trust for the Grand Master, and it is to be recommended that the Master be encouraged to address himself to rule 101 most carefully before he is installed into the chair of King Solomon.

The Warrant is of course the document which gives the authority to the Lodge in general and the Master in particular to Initiate, Pass and Raise Candidates for Freemasonry – without the Warrant the Lodge is not regular and ceremonies cannot be performed.

The question sometimes asked by lay brethren who see the Warrant of the Lodge framed and on show in a masonic hall 'how can the Master say I place in your hands the Warrant of the Lodge when it is fixed firmly to the wall of the Temple'?

A totally relevant question which can only be answered by the questioner allowing a free use of poetic licence, for the phrase used by the Master is one of free licence of the English language and should not be taken too literally. The author has on occasions heard the same phrase varied to the words 'I now place into your care (indicating with his hand its position on the Temple wall) the Warrant of the Lodge', this covers the situation equally well and does not offend the 'pure at heart'.

What then is the Centenary Warrant? Can this not be used in place of the Lodge Warrant issued when the Lodge was consecrated? The answer to that question is NO and the reason is simple, the Centenary Warrant is the 'official' proof that the Lodge has completed an unbroken period of one hundred years of activity and it permits the Lodge and all its members to wear a Centenary Jewel of the style and design emblazoned on the Centenary Warrant. You will of course now appreciate that to try to use the Centenary Warrant in place of the Lodge Warrant is completely wrong and and should never be permitted, and more to the point the Lodge is not regular!

The same comments of course apply equally to a Bi-Centenary Warrant, the purpose of which is to authorise the wearing of a bar on the Centenary Jewel with the engrossment 'CC' signifying two hundred years of continuous working.

Chapter Nineteen

The Worshipful Master

WE HAVE already covered elsewhere the subject of 'Training the Master Elect' and 'The Festive Board' so what is there left to say on the subject of the Worshipful Master?

There are some basic points which have not so far been considered in this book and it is important that we now turn to the overall management of the Lodge and its Committees and members.

We are, for the purposes of simplicity, not mentioning here the subject of proficiency in the ritual, control of the Festive Board, or the Training of the Master Elect. We shall however deal with those matters which are not usually dealt with in masonic books on 'how to do this or that'.

Let us first look at the overall control of the Lodge meeting, The Master of course, knows well in advance the Ceremony he will be performing and whether he will be carrying this out in full, or perhaps sharing a part or parts of it with other Brethren. We would make a basic point at this time, we all have differing concentration abilities and whilst some Brethren can perform perfectly a two hour meeting without any type of assistance, others are not so capable and are both mentally and physically strained after an hour or even less of total concentration.

Remember when a Past Master accepts the gavel and takes the chair to perform a ceremony at the invitation of the Worshipful Master he does NOT wear the collar of the Worshipful Master.

Remember also that the Master should sit on the IMMEDIATE left of the Past Master who has been so invited to perform the ceremony.

The second point to be made is that unless the brother performing the ceremony is particularly gifted with a voice filled with interest, tone, and delightful diction, it is highly likely that the

Brethren would welcome a change of Orator after a period of one hour has passed, possibly even before. The point we make here, is think the meeting through from the standpoint of those who have to listen not just those who are asked to 'stand and deliver'.

The more Brethren you can involve in the work of the Lodge the better, for they will have a reason for attending and bringing guests. Such involvement is the sign of a thinking Master who wishes to have a happy lodge for all his Brethren not just for himself during his year in the chair of King Solomon.

Try, if possible, and time permits during the year, to introduce a little education into the Lodge meeting. A short paper, an article from a masonic magazine, some questions and answers from research sources will all help to break what is so frequently called the one, two three, installation, mentality.

Variety so it is said is the spice of life. The Brethren will welcome the chance to listen to something different and a Master could well be remembered as one who thought very carefully about his year before he got there rather than carrying out the list of ceremonies placed before him by Brother Secretary.

A variation on the normal procedure in a lodge is to hold once a year a Past Masters' night at which the Past Masters' of the Lodge occupy the offices usually held by junior brethren and perform various parts of the ceremony. This assists in keeping the interest and enthusiasm of the Past Masters' albeit but once a year.

One of the oddities of Masonic elevation is the assumption that simply because a brother has reached the chair of his Lodge he is necessarily competent and skilled in the art of Chairmanship of the Lodge committees in which he will, by virtue of his Mastership have cause to run and control.

How then does the Master achieve such experience, and where and when should he endeavour to expand his experience so that on assuming the chair of King Solomon he can carry out his duties with distinction at any committee he is asked to 'Chair'?

The answer must of necessity cover it wide ranging group of exposures and opportunities. Most Lodges, within their Lodge management structure, include the Wardens as part of the overall committee and the two years of attending meetings will give him a chance to listen and learn from at least two predecessors. He should remember that being Chairman is a totally different role to perform from that of a Committee member. To 'Chair' any meeting successfully you must ensure that every participant is given the opportunity to make his contribution and not allow 'the few' to dominate the meeting which will frequently happen without the careful control exercised by the capable Chairman. Where direction is needed the wise Chairman will give that assistance clearly and concisely, he should endeavour to keep any discussion clearly 'on line' and not allow it to wander off the main issues being discussed.

The Chairman should, if such is necessary, keep a few notes in front of him in order that if a summary of the meeting is required later, he can give that summary, clearly and concisely in order that all participants are aware of the points discussed prior to a decision being made on any particular subject.

Where a Candidate for Initiation is being interviewed the Chairman (the Master) should always explain who he is and introduce the other members of the Committee not necessarily by name but by general terminology such as 'I am the Master of the Lodge and my name is . . . the brethren seated around the table are the Past Masters and Committee members of the Lodge'.

The Director of Ceremonies can assist very considerably in making quite sure that the Master, prior to his Chairing his first meeting is well trained in what he has to do, when he has to do it, and how he has to do it. First impressions are very important for they are frequently those which remain with us for the rest of our masonic careers and the unsure Master chairing his Committee meeting badly will create an unfortunate image for his Lodge which he and the members will regret.

Take every opportunity to gain experience by studying the manner and style which others use in Chairing a meeting. You will be quite surprised at the different styles which are used but the best by far is that which leaves the members feeling they have said all they wished to say, that the Chairman did not impose his will on the meeting and that the summing up was both fair and accurate.

Chairing the Ladies' Night is another meeting for which little training takes place but on this occasion your main duty is to ensure you meet everyone, make sure you have a speech of welcome and thanks, and ensure that you do not spend your evening talking Lodge business, for this is the evening on which

Lodge business should be completely forgotten and the Ladies cared for to the exclusion of all else.

The Master of his Lodge will undoubtedly receive many invitations to attend other meetings during the course of his year in the chair. He should therefore be ready to reply to the invitation to speak on behalf of the guests for he will almost certainly be asked as a visiting Master to do so.

The wise Master will have two or three different speeches ready in advance so that when the occasion arises he does not feel a terrible sense of panic. Remember the old Boy Scout motto 'Be Prepared'.

Chapter Twenty

The Tyler

THE TYLER or Outer Guard is of course the first person most Candidates meet on the day that their Initiation takes place. He must therefore be a brother of caring disposition and good organisation for it is he and no other who will prepare the Candidate for what is probably one of the most important days in his life.

Tylers by their very nature are frequently of mature years, knowledgeable, and time-serving brethren who have agreed to be of service to lodges other than their own in officiating as the Tyler to your Lodge. Their work includes guarding the exterior of the Lodge, the announcing of Visiting Brethren, the preparation of Candidates, and the general care of the equipment of the Lodge.

Tylers will frequently provide aprons for those taking their Third Degree, for the Master on the night of his Installation and generally provide at the request of the Committee of Management such items as are required from time to time to make certain that the lodge operates in an efficient manner.

The Tyler will lay out the Lodge to the best of his ability prior to the commencement of the meeting and will ensure that he has the correct name and title of all Candidates for the ceremonies, whom he will of course have to announce later. The Tyler is in many cases a paid official and it is therefore essential that Brother Treasurer keeps himself informed of the current rates of remuneration in order that a good Tyler is not lost for want of a little thought about his rate of pay.

The working relationship between the Director of Ceremonies and the Tyler is a most important one for as is described in detail in Chapter Two, the Director of Ceremonies relies very much on the work of the Tyler in laying out the Lodge correctly although, and we do not apologise for repeating this statement, the responsibility for the correct layout of the Lodge and the checking that all the equipment required for the work during the afternoon and evening is present, is entirely that of the Director of Ceremonies not the Tyler.

The Tyler as we all know plays an important part for the Lodge at the Festive Board by giving the final toast of the evening to 'All poor and distressed Freemasons' – 'wishing them a speedy relief from their suffering and a safe return to their native land should they so desire'.

This last paragraph is included to remind Directors of Ceremonies that the Tyler should NEVER use the Master's gavel when carrying out this final toast of the evening.

In most lodges the Tyler comes into the Lodge but once a year on the occasion of his Investiture at the Installation Meeting. It is a very nice gesture on the part of the Worshipful Master (after he has invested the Tyler with his Collar) to say a few kind words about his service to the Lodge, which, for the most part takes place out of sight of the Brethren both before and after they have arrived and departed from the Lodge Room and the Festive Board.

The Director of Ceremonies can assist in this small but important courtesy by reminding the Master of this gesture during the rehearsal prior to the meeting taking place.

The Tyler is an elected official and as the *Book of Constitutions* states his election must take place on the occasion of the duly proscribed election meeting as stated in the By-Laws of the Lodge. In most Lodges this is the meeting immediately preceding the Installation Meeting itself.

A Tyler unable to be present at the Installation can of course be invested at the next most convenient meeting, but what is the situation if the Tyler finds that between the Election meeting and the Installation meeting he is not able to accept the office either now or in the future? The *Book of Constitutions* is quite clear that the Tyler being an elected office as well as a regular office, it is unconstitutional for the Lodge to meet without a Tyler. The simple answer is for the Master to ask a Past Master to act as Tyler for the opening of the Lodge and at the earliest opportunity 'appoint' another Past Master from the Lodge as Tyler which for the unbelieving is perfectly in order. For proof read rule 113 of the *Book of Constitutions* which states:–

'The Tyler shall be elected by the members on the regular day of election of the Master. A Lodge, however, may resolve that a subscribing member of the Lodge shall be Tyler without emolument, in which case he shall be appointed with the other Officers by the Master.'

There can be little doubt that a Lodge finding itself in such a predicament would willingly support the Master's suggestion that a Past Master be appointed to this important and very necessary office.

Chapter Twenty One

Danger Signals

WHAT ON earth can this chapter contain we can hear you say. Well, read on, for what is spoken of here is of interest to every Director of Ceremonies and Preceptor of a Lodge of Instruction. The points which are raised in this chapter are of vital importance to all who care about the future of their lodge and the retention of its members, for it concerns the two most frequent occasions that are most likely to cause a loss of members.

Upon his Initiation the newly received Candidate is the centre of attention. He receives many congratulations on the night of his entry into the Craft and is made to feel the most important person in the Lodge, and in truth that is precisely what he is on that night.

As time passes he continues to be the focus of attention both by his learning the questions from one degree to another then undertaking that degree, finally arriving at the point where he is made a Master Mason. He continues as a focal point in the Lodge for the best part of a year to eighteen months and then he reaches the first of the two danger points in his life in the Lodge.

Sad to say, after so much attention the new member finds a period in his membership which is fallow. He is no longer the centre of attention, that has passed to some other newly Initiated Brother or Brethren and he is now three or four years away from being invested as a Steward of the Lodge.

Watch for the signs of 'DANGER', they start with a dropping off of his attendance at the Lodge of Instruction, then a missed Lodge meeting or two, then absences without a reason being tendered, followed by a non-payment of his annual subscription, then cessation of membership, or even worse an exclusion from the Lodge under Rule 148. That is the sequence and it happens more often than you think.

How then does this situation occur and what is the answer to the problem as outlined above.

Surprisingly the answer is very simple indeed, it is to ensure that all Brethren, particularly those in their first few years of membership are properly integrated into the Lodge and above all made to feel wanted, and necessary to the total operation of the Lodge. The Proposer and Seconder of every Candidate into the Craft will be able to determine that this feeling of warmth and well being will prevail and the Candidate, now of course a fully fledged member, feels a sense of importance in the Lodge.

This can be achieved in a number of ways. One such is to give the member a role to play within the Lodge. Get him to learn the Charge after Initiation, or some other significant piece of ritual, in other words involve him in the affairs of the Lodge. Arrange with the Master for this Brother to be able to deliver that piece of ritual at a regular Lodge meeting. Show him you are interested in his membership and will continue to be, for the rest of his masonic career.

Here we would remind the Proposer and Seconder that their involvement with the Candidate does not end when the night of his Initiation has arrived and passed into history. It does in fact begin on the occasion that they signed his application form and continues for the rest of the masonic life of the Brother they chose to bring into the Craft.

There can scarcely, be a sadder answer to the question asked about the absence of a recently Initiated Brother than for the Proposer or Seconder to say 'I don't know why he is not here'. Who should know better than his Proposer or Seconder? It is their responsibility and theirs alone. They must take a continuing interest in him. Watch for this DANGER time for it happens far more often than you think.

Now for the second DANGER period in the masonic life of the Lodge member.

Once a Brother starts at the bottom of the Stewards' list and progresses through to the first of his offices on the floor of the Lodge as Inner Guard he gains a certain momentum, and with it a sense of involvement and a future within the Lodge, and so it continues right up to his Mastership.

Following his year in charge of 'everything' to do with the

Lodge he then undertakes probably the most difficult year of his masonic career to date, namely the year he spends as Immediate Past Master.

Quite suddenly when that year comes to an end, the Immediate Past Master finds himself after some ten or twelve years in the spotlight of the affairs of the Lodge, no longer being consulted by anyone on anything. There is not even a word of thanks to him on the night that he ceases to be the Immediate Past Master of the Lodge.

Suddenly he has become, overnight, a nobody, his opinion is not sought, he has no role to perform, all the senior offices are filled with capable brethren and he is just another Past Master without a job. His elevation to Provincial or District rank is not going to arrive for possibly another eight to ten years so how does he adjust to his new non-starring role?

Sadly, if he is not looked after very carefully at this stage in his masonic career he can, and frequently does, find pastures new to conquer. There are, as we know, always offices to be filled and new rituals to learn in the side degrees the advocates of which are always keen to attract new members where a real and useful role can be offered to them and where they can be made to feel needed and necessary once again.

How then do we overcome this particular problem for it does and will continue to arise every year and surely there can never be enough offices for all the Past Masters to occupy?

Elsewhere in this book we have discussed the advisability of the Treasurer, Secretary, and Director of Ceremonies standing down from office every five to seven years. Clearly if this is carried out then virtually every other year a senior office will become vacant and a Past Master without office can be invested and made to feel necessary once again. What of the others? Let us remember that the Almoner, Charity Steward, and Assistant Secretary are all very necessary offices in the Lodge and require much dedication and effort if they are to be performed efficiently.

Catering for Past Masters in this manner will avoid the danger of the Lodge losing a keen and enthusiastic brother simply because 'there is nothing for him to do'.

It is a fallacy to believe that the offices of Treasurer, Secretary and Director of Ceremonies have to be held by brethren for year after year and are only relinquished when the brother holding the office signifies he has reached the point of no return and the lodge honours the brother holding the office for twenty-five years. What absolute nonsense! This brother has very probably been the root cause of many capable Past Masters leaving the Lodge over those twenty-five years simply because he would not 'move over' to let another brother show his worth. No matter how capable you are, remember that no brother is irreplaceable and he might even be doing his Lodge a disservice by remaining in office when quite obviously the time has arrived for him to go.

Think on these things.

Chapter Twenty Two

Consecrations

THE CONSECRATION of a Lodge is strictly the responsibility of the United Grand Lodge of England but in Provinces and Districts it is delegated to the Provincial or District Grand Master. The ceremony is almost universally the same throughout the Provinces and Districts of the United Grand Lodge of England with small local variations only being permitted.

The ceremony begins with the incoming procession into the lodge which is opened in the three degrees and the Consecrating Officer addresses the brethren on the purpose of the meeting and calls for the opening prayer. An Oration is usually given by the Provincial or District Grand Chaplain which is then followed by the Dedication Prayer, leading to the Invocation, at which point the lodge board is uncovered and the Elements of Consecration are carried round the lodge.

It should be mentioned here that wherever possible a copy of the Chaplain's Oration should be obtained for the lodge records.

Hymns are sung, Corn is scattered and Wine and Oil are poured. The Petitioners of the Lodge are arranged in order and Salt is scattered or, in some cases, placed on the left shoulders of the Petitioners.

The Lodge is then Dedicated by the Consecrating Officer.

Next the Lodge is Constituted and the Patriarchal Blessing is given. This part of the ceremony being completed the care of the Lodge is frequently handed over to the Deputy Provincial or District Grand Master who carries out the ceremony of Installing the first Master of the new Lodge. Usually such an occasion takes about three hours from start to finish depending upon the length of the Oration and the number of Founders participating in the ceremony.

It is quite usual for the Petitioners, as they are known prior to the Lodge being Consecrated, to be rehearsed in the various parts they have to play in the ceremony prior to the day or on the day itself by the Provincial or District Grand Director of Ceremonies. The rehearsal of a full Consecration ceremony is deprecated by the United Grand Lodge of England by anyone other than those who are to perform the ceremony itself and it should certainly never be rehearsed in a private Lodge of Instruction.

There are many things an enthusiastic group of Petitioners can do to assist themselves on the day of the Consecration. If you should be appointed as Director of Ceremonies designate of this new Lodge you will probably have a more than average amount of work to do in bringing brethren from various masonic ritual backgrounds into an agreed form of ceremonial for the lodge.

It is important at this stage of the development that variations are not allowed to creep into the working that has been agreed upon.

If a particular form of ritual has been decided upon then it should be adhered to without demure by all the Petitioners. Once a small variation is granted to some well meaning brother others will automatically follow and you will have a spurious form of ritual which will be understood by no one and which will also be impossible to teach at a later stage when you have a regular Lodge of Instruction in existence and a group of newly initiated brethren to teach. Be firm at the start and you will carry the day and be thanked in the future by all concerned. After all you did not take the job to be popular did you?

Remember that Consecrations are busy days for everyone. An early attendance is essential and several meetings of the Petitioners prior to the day of Consecration are to be recommended. Planning of every item in fine detail is essential from car parking, through to changing rooms for the various brethren attending, the ceremonial itself, the dining facilities, the serving of wine and the care of the guests.

Also arrangements must be made for presenting the Founders to the Consecrating Officer, the speeches at the Festive Board, getting the autographs of the team of Consecrating Officials for the lodge records, as it will be difficult if not impossible to get them after the day is over.

Has a photographer been booked to take those most important post Consecration pictures? If so has the Provincial or District

Director of Ceremonies been advised in order that he can be sure the Consecrating Officer and his team will remain fully clothed in their masonic regalia until the photographer is ready for the sitting to commence.

Simple things can help the day to be a success, planning the seating of all the guests and telling them their seat numbers well before the day itself will get one problem dealt with in advance. Checking that all the regalia is obtained well before the day of the Consecration, check it thoroughly to ensure that all the Collar Jewels are what were ordered. Have you obtained a Warrant Case, Cuffs for the Master and Wardens, Wands for the Director of Ceremonies, Assistant Director of Ceremonies and Deacons and have they been placed ready for use when the moment arrives?

Have Founder's Jewels been obtained? If they have it is normal practice for them to be displayed once the Consecrating Officer has presented the newly Installed Master with his Founder's Jewel. At this point in the ceremony the Brethren can now affix their own jewels in place.

Consecration ceremonies vary from Province to Province and District to District, but they all have a central theme which is varied according to the number of Officers participating in the Provincial or District team.

In London the team of Consecrating Officers is generally smaller than that used in a Province or District but the ceremony itself is virtually identical.

Consecration ceremonies can truthfully be said to be the birth of a lodge and they are occasions for much celebration for they bring to a fitting end the planning, waiting, organising and hoping which goes into the Founding of a new lodge usually spanning at least two years from inception to Consecration.

Chapter Twenty Three

The Banner Dedication

THE OCCASION may well arise when a Lodge Banner is either commissioned or presented to the Lodge and the official Dedication of that Banner is then requested of the Province or District. The day is fixed and the arrangements are made for a rehearsal, possibly before the day of the meeting but most usually on the day itself. How then can the Director of Ceremonies help his Lodge by being ready for the occasion with his brethren properly trained in what they have to do?

With only very slight alterations the format as shown below will be that most frequently used and it is perfectly permissible for the ceremony to be rehearsed prior to the day in order that the officiating Director of Ceremonies from the Province or District will only have to 'fine tune' the local arrangements made.

The Conducting of a Banner Dedication in a Private Lodge

The Past Masters' and Brethren of the Lodge should be ranged on either side of the Lodge from the Senior Deacon down and from the Assistant Director of Ceremonies down. Ideally all seats should be ticketed with the name of the person to whom the seat is allocated.

The holder which is to receive the Banner should be placed at an angle between the Chaplain and the Lodge Director of Ceremonies. It should be easily accessible from either side to allow the Provincial or District Grand Director of Ceremonies access to the back to support the holder whilst the unveiling takes place.

Make sure that the Banner Pole will fit the Holder

Make sure that the Banner can be unveiled without difficulty

Check that the BANNER IS OUTSIDE THE LODGE at the start of the meeting.

Seating from the Worshipful Master to his right as viewed from the front should be the Immediate Past Master, Provincial or District Chaplain, Lodge Chaplain. To the left of the Worshipful Master as viewed from the front is the Provincial or District Grand Master (hereafter referred to as the Dedicating Officer) and other Grand Officers in order of rank.

The Provincial or District Grand Director of Ceremonies should sit in the chair usually occupied by the Senior Deacon who should move down one seat towards the West.

At the appropriate moment the Worshipful Master will say 'Brother Director of Ceremonies will you please retire with the Banner Party'.

The Lodge Director of Ceremonies then stands and moves to the centre of the Lodge in front of the Worshipful Master and says 'Will the brethren designated as the Banner Party please stand' When this has been done he says 'Please follow the Assistant Director of Ceremonies and me from the Lodge', or some other appropriate words of command.

When the Inner Guard signifies to the Worshipful Master that the Banner Party are ready to enter the Lodge the Worshipful Master says 'Brethren we will now sing "O God Our Help in Ages Past"'. Once the Organist has started to play the Hymn the Banner Party should enter in two columns with the exception that the Banner is central between two brethren in the front of the procession each of whom will be directing the Banner Holder by gripping his left and right elbows respectively. (Do remember that the Banner Holder cannot see where he is going since the Banner is directly in front of his face).

When the last verse of the hymn is started the brethren in the Banner Party should fill in from the back making a number of rows of four with the exception of the front row which remains at three. This must be completed by the end of the hymn but there is no need to rush for there is plenty of time to complete this action.

The Lodge Director of Ceremonies then asks the Worshipful Master to accept the Banner on behalf of the Past Masters and Brethren of the ... Lodge No. 0000. The Worshipful Master replies and asks the Provincial or District Grand Chaplain to give the Opening Prayer. At this point the Provincial or District Grand Director of Ceremonies says 'To order Brethren for the Opening Prayer', giving the sign of reverence.

When this is completed the Worshipful Master asks the Director of Ceremonies to see that the Banner is placed in position.

When this has been done the Lodge Director of Ceremonies and the Banner Holder go back to their original positions. (It is usual for the Banner Holder to require some assistance in placing the Banner Pole in position).

The Worshipful Master then turns to the Dedicating Officer and asks him to unveil the Banner to which he receives an affirmative response.

The Provincial or District Director of Ceremonies then gives a court bow to the Dedicating Officer but precedes him to the back of the Banner and whilst holding the pole very firmly with his hand also places his foot on the base to support the pole whilst the unveiling actually takes place.

When ready he should signify to the Dedicating Officer that he may proceed.

After this has been done the Dedicating Officer then says 'I now call upon the Provincial or District Grand Chaplain for the Dedication Prayer', the Provincial or District Grand Director of Ceremonies then says 'To order Brethren for the Dedication Prayer' and gives the sign of reverence.

After the prayer has been completed the Provincial or District Grand Director of Ceremonies then gives a Court bow to the Dedicating Officer returning him to his seat, and then says, 'Be Seated Brethren' (he does not sit himself and neither does the Dedicating Officer). All should sit and the Banner Party also will resume their places and sit. When all are seated the Dedicating officer says 'I now call upon the Provincial or District Grand Chaplain for the Oration'. Both the Dedicating Officer and the Provincial or District Grand Director of Ceremonies then sit.

After the Oration is completed the Worshipful Master says 'we shall now sing the hymn. Now thank we all our God', when this is finished the Provincial or District Grand Director of Ceremonies says 'To Order Brethren for the Patriarchal Benediction' showing the sign of reverence. When this is over he says 'Be Seated Brethren'.

Remember to tell the Organist that he will be required to play 'So Mote It Be' after each Hymn and each Prayer.

Finally the Worshipful Master then rises firstly to thank the Dedicating Officer for coming to unveil and dedicate the Banner, and the Provincial or District Grand Chaplain for his 'interesting and stimulating' Oration.

The occasion of a Banner Dedication is a very special meeting and the normal workload should be as light as possible in order that the focus of the day can be upon the Dedicating of the new Lodge Banner.

Just as a small reminder to the Director of Ceremonies; if you wish to have photographs taken not only of the Banner but of the Dedicating team as well, this should be organised with the knowledge that the usual time taken for the complete Banner Dedicating ceremony is between twenty and thirty minutes.

Banners require special care if their life span is to be maximised. Do ensure that your Tyler is properly instructed in the correct manner of carrying the Banner from the Locker room and also in its careful storage between the meetings of the Lodge.

Banners are also very expensive to make and costly to replace, therefore make absolutely certain that your Lodge Banner has a suitable cover to protect it between meetings and that its value is correctly assessed for insurance purposes.

Chapter Twenty Four

The Undesirable D.C.

VERY EARLY in this book we mentioned the totally undesirable Director of Ceremonies who is highly visible, very vocal and who plays a much higher profile role than his office in the lodge either requires or needs. Too much of this high profile behaviour can demean a Master's performance, overshadow the work of all the Officers and generally undermine the enthusiasm and dedication of younger brethren. Not only is such a Director of Ceremonies undesirable he is to be deprecated in fullest measure, for he can, if allowed free reign, bring a good lodge to its knees. How then do we handle such a situation if it exists and more to the point how do we stop such a situation from developing?

The common thread which runs through all dictatorial Directors of Ceremonies is the lack in receiving correct training themselves and secondly and most generally being allowed to serve too long in office.

Let us take the first point made, that of receiving correct training. Sadly many Directors of Ceremonies believe that a strong full voice a mildly dominating manner and the belief that everything they say and do is absolutely right and that any question that they may be wrong or even slightly misinformed is a declared insult.

Yes we have all met them, have we not? The sad thing is that to a man they all have the interests of the lodge so much at heart that they cannot believe they could possibly be the reason for its demise or for the unhappiness of its brethren.

Since there is probably very little that can be done about the training of the Director of Ceremonies after he is found to be amongst those whom we have described as undesirable, we should therefore concentrate on the second factor namely that of length of service.

Clearly it can be established that upon appointment the new incumbent was certainly not the tyrant we now see as having developed after some years in the office. How then did this metamorphosis take place? Surprisingly the answer is very often staring you right in the face in the form of insecurity, or in some cases an inferiority complex.

Very occasionally we see a Director of Ceremonies shouting and generally making his presence felt, due to the possibility (in his eyes) that the brethren will not do as they are asked if this is done in a gentle manner, so he resorts to the loud voice with a slightly implied hint that if all do not do as they are told there will be some sort of trouble.

This can well come from a direct doubt in the mind of the Director of Ceremonies as to the correct course of action to take. After all a confident brother has no need to raise his voice has he? He knows he is right and therefore quietly asks for the cooperation of the brethren in carrying out any particular action. Remember the ideal Director of Ceremonies is one who has steadily built his knowledge by the means of understudying a worthy and proven Director of Ceremonies and by questions, study and watching a variety of experienced Directors of Ceremonies in action.

All too often the noisy Director of Ceremonies has taken the job when no one else could be found to fill the role, or has had no prior experience in the work of the Director of Ceremonies and has taken his entire store of knowledge from the work of another Director of Ceremonies or Directors of Ceremonies in other lodges who perhaps use totally different workings from that used in your lodge.

What then can we do to alleviate such a situation once it has arisen? There are in fact many things one can do, ranging from replacing the Director of Ceremonies completely without warning which will undoubtedly cause factions to arise in the Lodge and this is of course to be avoided. All changes of the senior officers in the lodge should in an ideal world be planned, known to the incumbent and the replacement well in advance of such a change taking place.

Another course of action is for the Director of Ceremonies to be confronted with the dissatisfaction of the brethren and asked to behave in a more reasonable manner in his work in the lodge. This course of action can and probably will bring forward a storm of denial and the fact that he is not understood, and look how much time he has given to the lodge etc. etc. The list will be almost endless, including most probably the fact that the brethren are very ungrateful for his years of loyal service.

How then should this difficult situation be addressed? The answer is really very simple, it is to play to the vanity of such a person by calling for his advice, assistance and help. Thus you are then both metaphorically sitting on the same side of the desk not confronting each other across it!

Try this as an opening remark, 'Some of the Past Masters and I have been talking about the future of the lodge and the manner in which we can use our younger Past Masters to maximum advantage and this of course means we must look at all the offices in the lodge particularly the more senior offices and ensure that no one stays in office too long, so that everyone can feel needed and necessary, and perhaps even more importantly that we retain their membership'.

This opening gambit must provoke a response which will almost certainly be connected with his own role in the subject you are discussing.

Another method is to bring the subject around to the future and who the Director of Ceremonies sees taking over from him and when does he see that happening? Does he see the replacement mentioned as his ideal choice? And what does he look for in the man who is to succeed him, always remembering that for him to retire whilst still being available for advice, consultation, and assistance should such be needed is a distinct benefit for the Lodge.

To try to get a time serving Director of Ceremonies to change his ways after many years of service is a very difficult if not impossible task and very often the only course is to find a new Director of Ceremonies. There is however the occasional opportunity to put right the errors of years but this does of course require the right situation, the right time and the right ambience in which to present to the erring Director of Ceremonies the objections and behaviour patterns which have served to aggravate and annoy the brethren over many years.

It is very important that any such discussion is conducted on a one to one basis for a third person creates an audience to whom the natural objections of the Director of Ceremonies can be directed. One to one and start with the concerns of the brethren for the abstract, the lodge, the overall happiness of the brethren and the guests who have made comments. Never under any circumstances say 'Well Brother so and so said'. This personalises such comments and the direction of the conversation is completely lost.

State the points you wish to make more in the manner of questions such as 'Why do we do this or that, and why in that particular manner?' Such a comment will provoke an answer which can then be discussed in detail. This is the appropriate time to raise another point of view particularly if it is one about which the brethren of the lodge have strong feelings. We do so hope that the point of this section is not lost on the reader, for what we are seeking to do is to re-direct an enthusiastic brother into the thinking of the majority of the lodge whose wishes should always be not only considered but observed.

Confrontation will seldom work. Joint discussion in the right way in the right setting – by the right person – will usually work far better than might be imagined particularly if a slow, controlled voice is used whilst the discussion is progressing. A raised voice will do no more than beget another raised voice, almost certainly to no avail.

Chapter Twenty Five

Provincial or District Grand Lodge Meetings

THIS CHAPTER is primarily for those Provincial Officers who are charged with the running of a Provincial or District Grand Lodge Meeting which is usually the annual occasion at which the Brethren of the Province or District are invested by the Provincial or District Grand Master with their new Provincial or District Grand Rank.

Planning for an occasion as important as this must of necessity start many months ahead and it requires the involvement of many of the senior Provincial or District Grand Officers. The Provincial or District Grand Secretary having arranged the venue and the Festive Board (if there is to be one), the Provincial or District Grand Treasurer for obvious reasons has to be consulted in regard to the financial outlay involved, and the Provincial or District Grand Director of Ceremonies for the organisation, planning and overall effective running of the meeting itself.

Once the brethren to be so honoured are known, the usual three groups fall into, Active, Promotions, and Past Ranks and seating tickets should be prepared when all the acceptances are received from the brethren to be so honoured.

Seating lists have now to be prepared in both chronological rank order for presenting to the presiding officer and also in alphabetical order for ease of answering the many questions from brethren who wish to know their seats on the day.

Many copies of these lists should be produced and displayed in areas adjacent to the Temple to be used for the Investiture. This action will help, although not totally dispose of the requirement to have an ample supply of Ushers in the Temple itself. Also, copies of the seating lists at the point of signing in for the meeting make it possible for questions from enquiring brethren to be answered swiftly.

Those receiving Active Rank will be required to collect their Jewel of office and should be directed to a totally separate signing in point where they can sign for the safety of the Jewel with which they are to be invested. These jewels will have to be returned to the Province or District in time for the following year's Provincial or District Grand Lodge meeting.

The Provincial or District Grand Secretary will, a short time prior to the meeting advise the Provincial or District Grand Director of Ceremonies of the names and ranks of the V.I.P., visiting brethren in order that the visitors, incoming procession as well as seating on the dais can be arranged.

Here you must make quite certain that you plan this action very carefully, always ensuring from the Provincial or District office of the Province or District from which a particular VIP brother is coming that his current rank is . . . as he may not now be at the rank shown in the Masonic Year Book having perhaps been promoted at the last Annual Investiture of Grand Lodge.

When you have assured yourself that you have the correct ranks of everyone coming to the meeting you must now ensure that within those ranks you have the year of appointment of each brother. Having completed that exercise you are now in a position to put together a processional plan into the Provincial Grand Lodge, together with its subsequent dais seating plan, in order that as the visiting V.I.P. brethren process into the lodge they will automatically fill the seats in the right order.

It is essential for the convenience of your guests that you provide not only a chart for such visiting brethren in the robing room but also that each visiting VIP should be given a small plan of his seat on the dais plus his position in the ingoing procession. Every VIP should also be provided with a Brochure of the Provincial or District meeting together with a note of his position at the Festive Board Top Table after the meeting.

If there is to be a reception for the V.I.P guests after the meeting and before the Festive Board ALL V.I.P. guests must be advised where this is occurring and how to get to the designated room or area.

Clearly the planning of the Festive Board itself will be organised by the Provincial or District office but it is essential that the Provincial or District Grand Director of Ceremonies knows just where everyone is seated in order that if his senior executive officers should wish to locate anyone, he can immediately advise them where such VIP brethren are seated.

The announcing of the entry of the Provincial or District Grand Master etc. etc. etc. will inevitably be made by a Deputy Provincial or District Grand Director of Ceremonies at which point the Prov or District Grand Director of Ceremonies will lead the incoming party to their seats. The request for silence for Grace to be said by the Provincial or District Grand Chaplain will now be made after which all will be requested to be seated.

During the course of the Dinner various toasts, individual to each Province and District will be made and those who are to speak will be introduced as at a normal Festive Board. The conclusion of the evening arrives at the point of the Provincial or District Grand Tyler's Toast.

It is always recommended that a debriefing meeting is held after a Provincial or District Grand Lodge to record those things which will require more or earlier attention next year and to examine if appropriate those areas of organisation which failed completely, or require rethinking in their entirety. This debriefing meeting brings forward many small points from which all concerned can learn and thus improve next year's planning and general organisation. Things to ask yourself after the Provincial or District Grand Lodge meeting are:–

a Did all organisation as planned, work satisfactorily?
b Was the timing of each part of the day correct?
c Did each Deputy G.D.C. fulfil his role correctly?
d Did each V.I.P. receive sufficient care and attention?
e Did the Ushers perform their duties correctly?
f Was the incoming procession correctly formed?
g Was the dais seating accurately arranged?
h Was the meeting itself correctly organised?
i Did the Investiture work efficiently?
j Was the Festive Board well organised?
k Did the Festive Board timing work?
l Were there any other points requiring attention?

Chapter Twenty Six

Your Successor

THE WISE Director of Ceremonies realises at a very early stage in his period of office that the day will come when he will either feel the need to retire, or that perhaps a future Master may prefer to have another Brother as his Director of Ceremonies rather than the current incumbent. Such is the right of every Master to do just that if he so desires.

The usual course of events in most lodges is for the Director of Ceremonies not only to advise the brethren when he feels the day is dawning for him to relinquish office but also to do so well in advance of his replacement taking over. In many cases the replacement Director of Ceremonies is the brother who has been acting as Assistant Director of Ceremonies for a number of years and is both well known for his ability and presence as well as his knowledge of the brethren and their capability, if called upon at short notice, to occupy an office.

Let us then take the case of a brother who has decided that the time has arrived for him to stand down from office at the next Installation Meeting what then should be his course of action?

As with the three principal offices in the Lodge, the Treasurer, Secretary and Director of Ceremonies it is always wise to alert the Past Masters to the situation in order that a form of general awareness and agreement prevails.

It must be accepted that at all times the decision regarding the appointment of the Director of Ceremonies is the total prerogative of the Master Elect when duly elected to that office. Such then must be the tentative approach of the Director of Ceremonies that general agreement to his successor is elicited from the Master Elect, for the main requirement at this time is the retention of the goodwill of the brethren and the confidence of the Past Masters to this newly proposed appointment.

If such is forthcoming then all is well and the present incumbent can immediately commence the process of handing over his role to his successor. Not infrequently it has been noted that a time serving Director of Ceremonies will spend a year as Assistant Director of Ceremonies after standing down from office if for no other reason than to assist his replacement in the first year of settling down into a new role.

The newly installed Master should ensure that the retiring Director of Ceremonies is suitably thanked for his years of service to the Lodge just prior to his successor being invested.

What however if such an ideal hand-over is not to be accomplished and the current incumbent is not willing to stand down on his own volition and has to be effectively 'removed from office' by the incoming Master?

Should such a sad situation exist one can only prevail on the good nature of the current Director of Ceremonies to think of the lodge rather than himself. In such cases there is usually a raised adrenalin level and a goodly proportion of pride being hurt. A small retirement present goes some way to heal such feelings.

A lesson should always be learned from a situation of this type and the Lodge itself should institute an understanding amongst its members that in an ideal arrangement the principal officers should change say every five to seven years so that no one officer gets to feel he is irreplaceable.

The ideal Director of Ceremonies and of course this is you is it not, will know, in advance that he is not doing the Lodge any service by continuing in office and that it is his duty, yes duty, to ensure that a suitable replacement takes over from him and then discuss this privately with the brother most likely to be the next Master of the Lodge. In so doing he can be seen to be putting the Lodge first and thinking ahead. Such a Director of Ceremonies will be remembered long after his tenure in office has passed.

Remember that every Brother brings to any office both strengths and weaknesses and that it is not necessarily a weakness to carry out some action or other in a manner different from that to which you are accustomed.

It is just his way and is not necessarily wrong.

Chapter Twenty Seven

Processions

PROCESSIONS INTO the Lodge do not usually present any particular problem to the Director of Ceremonies, the same however cannot be said about the outgoing procession which frequently presents the new Director of Ceremonies with raised adrenalin and considerable uncertainty with regard to the precise format of senior brethren that the outgoing procession should contain.

The golden rule is never to have more people in the outgoing procession than remain in the Temple. Accepting that the Master and his Wardens and Deacons are in their usual places in the outgoing procession it is normally quite unnecessary to include anyone other than Grand Officers and Provincial or District Grand Officers. Some lodges include Past Masters of and in the Lodge, some include visiting Past Masters. it is of course entirely up, to the Director of Ceremonies of the lodge to decide who is and who is not included in the outgoing procession.

Visiting dignitaries should of course be included as should guest Speakers. If you should be honoured by the presence of a Right Worshipful brother it is usually courteous to mention him by name and rank. Ideally an outgoing procession should contain no more than twelve to twenty brethren.

One aspect of the outgoing procession from the lodge which has not been dealt with so far is that connected with the brethren holding higher ranks particularly if they honour your lodge in large numbers. Let us for example take a situation which does occur regularly in some lodges namely that of seven or so Right Worshipful Brethren being present and frequently the same number of Very Worshipful Brethren as well.

What should the Director of Ceremonies of the Lodge do in such a case. Most usually of course the representing officer if such is the case would have his own Director of Ceremonies in attendance upon him. Let us assume however that such is not the case in the example we are describing.

The answer is unusually simple. Once the outgoing procession has been formulated and the Master taken from his chair in the East and the Wardens have fallen in behind him the Lodge Director of Ceremonies should simply say 'accompanied by Right Worshipful Brethren, Very Worshipful Brethren and the Officers of the United Grand Lodge of England'. It really is as easy as that, the Right Worshipful Brethren and then the Very Worshipful Brethren will form themselves into two lines behind the Wardens, and the Grand Officers will fall in behind them. Your outgoing procession is complete.

Finally, where exactly should Grand Stewards be placed in the outgoing procession? The best answer that can be given is that which is contained in an answer by the then Grand Secretary RW Bro J.W. Stubbs PJGW to a question from the Provincial Grand Secretary of Devonshire in a letter dated 7 January 1970, from which we quote:

(a) A Past Grand Steward is not a Grand Officer and is therefore junior to anyone who is a Past Grand Officer.
(b) He ranks above all holders of L.G.R. and O.G.R., and above all Provincial and District Grand Officers outside their own Province or District. He also ranks above Provincial and District Grand Officers *in* their own Province or District *except* one specifically representing the Provincial/District Grand Master at a meeting (or, in my opinion, when any Provincial/District Grand Officers are in personal attendance, eg. as Wardens upon their Provincial or District Grand Master.

Directors of Ceremonies are reminded that the Grand Stewards of the year ARE Grand Officers and must therefore be treated as such. To those Directors of Ceremonies who are in any doubt regarding the status of a brother wearing a Grand Stewards Apron and wonder whether his is or is not an active Grand Steward, simply glance at the jewel affixed to the end of his collar. Plate 21 in the *Book of Constitutions* shows this in detail. Past Grand Stewards wear a locket as described in rule 245 *Book of Constitutions*.

Chapter Twenty Eight

Aprons

ONE MYTH which continues to be perpetuated is that a brother may not, even for a few seconds stand in a lodge without wearing an apron. The Senior Warden when instructed by the Worshipful Master to do so, invests the Candidate with his apron in each of the degrees. When investing in the first degree he has a simple task to perform. In the second and third degrees he has to remove one apron before investing the candidate with another. It is perfectly permissible for the Senior Warden to remove the former apron and then invest the candidate with his new rank. In many lodges the process of trying to tie the new badge of rank over the former apron frequently reduces the ceremony to something resembling a farce. There is no ruling which stipulates that a candidate has to be invested in this ridiculous manner and where it continues to occur it should be stopped without delay.

Frequently one will see a newly installed Master being invested with his apron which has not been adjusted prior to the ceremony taking place. The efficient Director of Ceremonies will always make certain that the new apron the Master is to receive has been correctly adjusted before the start of the meeting.

Chapter Twenty Nine

Tracing Boards

We are all aware that there are three Tracing Boards used in the craft ceremonies and that they are changed as the Master moves from one degree to another, what is sometimes not appreciated is that it is perfectly permissible for the tracing board of the former degree to be retained on show whilst the lodge is in the higher degree.

There are many lodges who place their three tracing boards in front of the pedestals of the Junior Warden, Senior Warden, and Master respectively and once uncovered are left that way until the lodge is resumed in the lower degree when they are of course once again turned to face the pedestal.

Some Directors of Ceremonies are adamant that a tracing board of a lower degree must not be on show once the lodge has moved to a higher degree, such however is not the case.

Chapter Thirty

Balloting

DURING THE course of a masonic year the act of balloting in its various forms is used by every lodge. To the unthinking Director of Ceremonies this apparently simple procedure can be full of opportunities to fail and fail badly. Assuming the Master has declared the Ballot Box empty, the procedure would be:

Honorary Members

The *Book of Constitutions* rule 167 clearly states the manner in which the ballot for an Honorary Member must be conducted namely by individual ballot and be declared carried unless three or more black balls appear against it. It is therefore imperative that the brother who has been designated to deal with the allocation of ballot balls shall be instructed to place one ball only in the palm of each member of the lodge excluding of course existing Honorary Members. If the white and black ball system is being used obviously one ball of each colour should be handed to each member participating.

It is often the case that a brother who has not been so correctly instructed is seen to proffer to each member the bag of ballot balls from which any member could quite easily take two or three without anyone being aware. Such an action could easily lead to an unfair ballot with the resultant unhappiness within the lodge.

It is the duty of Directors of Ceremonies to ensure that they instruct those who are charged with this responsibility to carry it out in the manner described above.

The Worshipful Master and Treasurer

The usual manner of electing the Master and Treasurer is by written ballot, with the slips of paper being collected and handed to the Master for verification. It is totally unnecessary for the

Master, or anyone else to read out each slip of paper. All that the Master is required to do is to announce who received the majority of votes. It is not necessary for him to make mention of other names or spoiled ballot papers.

The use of the word unanimous is to be avoided, firstly because it is virtually an impossible statement to prove, and secondly because it is unnecessary to the proceedings for such a statement to be made.

The same comments apply equally to the ballot for the Treasurer.

The Tyler

The ballot for the Tyler is by a show of hands after a proposal which has been seconded has been made in open lodge. The Master should announce the result of the ballot which should then be recorded by Brother Secretary.

Initates and Joining Members

The same procedure is adopted as is used for the Honorary Member namely a choice of the yes or no drawer. Once again the brother handing the ballot balls to the lodge members should be very careful to ensure that each brother receives only one ball for each ballot unless of course the black and white ball system is being used.

Combined Balloting

It is perfectly permissible for a combined ballot to be taken for say a Joining Member and an Initiate. The United Grand Lodge of England recognises only 'candidates' not candidates for a specific reason ie Initiation or Joining. If as a result of a conjoint ballot being taken it proves not to be in favour, then a separate ballot must be taken immediately to determine the separate results.

Chapter Thirty One

The Assistant Director of Ceremonies

THE ROLE of Assistant Director of Ceremonies is frequently regarded as a sinecure to be given to a Past Master who is not looking for an office with much responsibility and who is quite happy to just be a helper to the Director of Ceremonies.

Such a view is both wrong and unthinking if believed by the Master Elect who of course is responsible for the appointment to office of the brother so selected. The duties of the Assistant Director of Ceremonies vary considerably according to the lodge. We would suggest that the following advice will assist the efficient Director of Ceremonies in the execution of his own duties.

The Assistant Director of Ceremonies should have clearly defined duties which are known and agreed by the Director of Ceremonies before the Assistant take up his new role.

During the usual lodge meeting he should take responsibility for the positioning of the kneeling stool for the candidate in the West and its removal afterwards. He should be responsible for greeting and seating all brethren below the rank of Worshipful Brother arriving after the meeting has commenced.

The transit of the apron for the candidate to the Senior Warden if taken from the East to the West can easily be left to the Assistant Director of Ceremonies. At the Installation Meeting the Assistant Director of Ceremonies can do much to ease the work of the Director of Ceremonies by collecting and handing to the Director of Ceremonies each collar as it is required together with the columns and gavels for the wardens, and the wands for the deacons.

The Assistant Director of Ceremonies should above all other duties ensure a standard of proficiency which will enable him to carry out the duties of the Director of Ceremonies should, for any reason, that officer be unable to be present.

It is frequently the case that the Assistant Director of Ceremonies is being considered for promotion to the rank of Director of Ceremonies. It is therefore essential that he is given the opportunity to perform various parts of the duties of the Director of Ceremonies throughout the year. He could be asked to form and control the outgoing procession from the lodge as part of that training. It would be perfectly acceptable for him to participate in the investiture of officers by presenting those below the junior deacon and also by escorting to and from their seats those Past Masters who are to deliver the three addresses.

Such active participation is to be encouraged. Training any officer for future service in the lodge shows sound forward thinking.

Chapter Thirty Two

The Royal Arch

THE WIDE coverage given to the duties of the Director of Ceremonies in the Craft Lodge apply equally to the Director of Ceremonies in a Royal Arch Chapter and it is therefore unnecessary for them to be repeated here.

There is far less ceremonial in a Royal Arch Chapter than that used in a lodge but the same attention to detail in regard to the pre-planning and overseeing of the work of the Janitor are needed if a trouble free meeting is to be held.

For the assistance of those Directors of Ceremonies charged with the responsibility for the correct laying out of the Royal Arch Temple a check list is included at the end of this book.

Chapter Thirty Three

A Touch on the Tiller

THE DIRECTOR of Ceremonies who has read this book and recognised himself throughout must be a very unusual man indeed. The paragon of virtue, blessed with the infinite Wisdom of Solomon and the tact and diplomacy of a United Nations Peacemaker, has yet to be moulded. So if you have by any chance felt that everything you do already in your lodge is exactly in line with what has been suggested, then we question why you bought the book in the first place, for you obviously did not need to do so. Perhaps someone tactfully gave it to you as a gift in the hope you would read it and who knows perhaps learn something!

It is of course much more likely that you have just been appointed to the office of Director of Ceremonies and wish to have a more general appraisal of the duties, as well as your general areas of operation within the Lodge, together with those things you can do to make the Lodge a happier more efficient place than perhaps you feel it is at this present time.

Remember that moderation in all things will make for a happy Lodge. Being right and letting everyone know it all the time is not only very irritating but it tends to make for an unhappy and fast diminishing number of Brethren in the Lodge.

The Director of Ceremonies should be the favourite uncle, the confident demonstrator of ceremonial, the guide and counsellor, the shoulder to lean on, the encouraging hand to Brethren lacking in confidence, and above everything always approachable and calm.

If he can portray those essential assets then he will succeed beyond his wildest dreams and, what is more, in the process become loved for his contribution to the happiness of the Brethren and that of the Lodge, to say nothing of Freemasonry Universal.

Appendix I

The ideal Lodge of Instruction annual plan of ceremonies with a graduated listing of offices being filled by a graduated team of brethren from Senior Warden through to the Sixth Steward occupying the Master's chair throughout the masonic season.

It is suggested that the officers of the lodge are listed in the order in which they appear on the lodge summons so that the Senior Warden is Bro 1, the Junior Warden is Bro 2 etc. etc. etc.

As will be seen from the listing below each officer is only scheduled to occupy those offices which are senior to him in the lodge. Officers nights which can be built into this plan will enable current officers to rehearse their role.

Date	Degree	WM	SW	JW	SD	JD	IG	Members
WK 1	FIRST	A	B	C	D	E	F	A = BRO 1
WK 2	SECOND	B	C	D	E	F	G	B = BRO 2
WK 3	THIRD	C	D	E	F	G	H	C = BRO 4
WK 4	FIRST	D	E	F	G	H	J	D = BRO 4
WK 5	SECOND	E	F	G	H	J	K	E = BRO 5
WK 6	THIRD	F	G	H	J	K	L	F = BRO 6
WK 7	FIRST	G	H	J	K	L	M	G = BRO 7
WK 8	SECOND	A	B	C	D	E	F	H = BRO 8
WK 9	THIRD	B	C	D	E	F	G	J = BRO 9
WK 10	FIRST	C	D	E	F	G	H	K = BRO 10
WK 11	SECOND	D	E	F	G	H	J	L = BRO 11
WK 12	THIRD	E	F	G	H	J	K	M = BRO 12
WK 13	FIRST	F	G	H	J	K	L	
WK 14	SECOND	G	H	J	K	L	M	

From Week 15 onwards the listing is simply repeated thereby giving a forty two week Lodge of Instruction plan. If you therefore multiply each officers place on the duty rota above by three you will see the opportunities each has to fulfil each office as listed. If the Lodge of Instruction has a regular attendance of more than twelve members then it is suggested that the work of the various offices is split during the ceremony thereby giving everyone present an opportunity to participate in the evening.

Appendix II

This is a check list for the Director of Ceremonies to use when a Lodge is to perform a ceremony of Initiation

Master's Pedestal
Senior Warden's Pedestal
Junior Warden's Pedestal
Three Tracing Boards
Rough & Perfect Ashlars
Tripod & Pulley Set
Volume of the Sacred Law
Square and Compasses
Box of Working Tools
Two Kneeling Stools
Glass of water for the Master
Officers Collars
Compasses for the Initiate
Plumb Rule for JW Pedestal
Gauntlets for WM, SW, JW
Passing Card for the Candidate
Three Gavels
Three Sounding Blocks
Senior and Junior Wardens Columns
Bible Cushion
Apron Cushion
Ballot Box
Ballot Balls
Banner (if appropriate)
E.A. Apron
Collection Bags
Alms Dish for JD
Poignard
Level for SW Pedestal
Four Wand Stands
Four Wands DC, ADC, SD, JD
Book of Const & By-Laws

....
....
....
....

If a ballot is to be taken the Director of Ceremonies must ensure that the ballot box is held completely level and not tilted to one side. It is equally democratic to vote against a proposition as to vote for it and members should not be influenced in the way in which they vote in a ballot.

For the election meeting it is very important that you ensure that the Brother Secretary has ready and available the slips of paper required for the voting to take place for the Master and the Treasurer. It is advisable that these are handed to the Deacons prior to the start of the meeting in order to save time and an unnecessary delay for the members.

Check list for the Second Degree

As per first degree list plus the following items
Square for use by SD on the Candidate
Square for use by the Inner Guard
Fellowcraft Apron
Raising card for the Candidate

Check list for the Third Degree

As per first degree plus the following items
Third Degree sheet
Compasses for the Inner Guard
Master Masons Apron
Ritual book for presentaton to the Candidate
Box of matches for relighting the candles
Hcavy Maul

Check list for the Installation Meeting

As per first degree list plus the following items
Collar Horse
Sword for the Tyler
Past Masters Collar and Collar Jewel for the Outgoing Master
Past Masters Breast Jewel (if applicable)

Appendix III

The following list is printed to enable those brethren who intend to progress through to the Master's Chair to have a plan of study over a seven year period. It shows what should be planned in each of those seven years leading to the Installation Meeting and the year as Master of the Lodge.

Year 1	When a Steward you should learn the First degree.
Year 2	When a Steward you should learn the Second degree and rehearse the First degree regularly.
Year 3	When the I.G. learn the charge after Initiation and rehearse the First and Second degrees regularly.
Year 4	When the J.D. learn the Third degree and rehease the First and Second degrees regularly.
Year 5	When the S.D. learn the Second degree tracing board and continue to rehearse the First, Second and Third degrees regularly.
Year 6	When the J.W. learn the Installation Ceremony and continue to rehearse the three degrees.
Year 7	When the S.W. learn the Investiture of Officers and continue to rehearse the three degrees.
Year 8	When the W.M. learn the Inner Working. Perform the ceremonies, Install your Successor and you will have a very happy, successful and memorable year as Master of your Lodge.

Appendix IV

This is a check list for the Director of Ceremonies to use when a Royal Arch Chapter is to perform a Ceremony of Exaltation.

Principals Robes, Sceptres, and Books.
Check the correct layout of the Principal Banners.
Check the correct layout of the Ensigns.
Check the layout of the Greater and Lesser Lights.
Check correct layout of Kneeling Stools.
Check correct layout of Plate and Triangle.
Check correct layout of Letters and Cover.
Check Robes for Scribes 'E' and 'N' and Sojourners.
Check Ballot Box and Ballot Balls.
Check Ballot Slips (election meetings only).
Check Bags for Charity Collection.
Check Hymn Cards.
Check Wands and Wand Stands for DC and ADC.
Glass of water for the MEZ.
Charter of the Chapter.
Book of Constitutions and By-Laws for the MEZ.
Collars for the following officers:

Scribe 'E'	Principals (3)	Organist
Scribe 'N'	I.P.Z.	Janitor
Treasurer	Stewards	1st Asst. Sojourner
D.C.	A.D.C.	2nd Asst. Sojourner
Principal Sojourner	Asst. Scribe 'E'	

Collar Horse (for installations only)
By-Laws for the Exaltee, and/or Joining Members.

....

....

....

....